The Mulligan Affair
Top Cop on the Take

Ian Macdonald
& Betty O'Keefe

CANADIAN CATALOGUING IN PUBLICATION DATA

Macdonald, Ian, 1928-
The Mulligan Affair

ISBN 1-895811-45-7

1. Mulligan, Walter
2. Police corruption—British Columbia—Vancouver
3. Vancouver (B.C.). Police Dept.—History
I. O'Keefe, Betty, 1930-
II. Title.
HV8160.V3M32 1997   364.1'323'0971133   C97-910628-1

First Edition 1997

Heritage House wishes to acknowledge the support of Heritage Canada, the British Columbia Arts Council and the Cultural Services Branch of the Ministry of Small Business, Tourism and Culture and BC Parks.

Cover, Book Design and Typesetting: Darlene Nickull
Edited by: Joanne Richardson

HERITAGE HOUSE PUBLISHING COMPANY LTD.
Unit #8 - 17921 55th Ave., Surrey, BC V3S 6C4

Printed in Canada

Dedication

This book is dedicated to the newsroom staffs at the *Vancouver Province* and the *Vancouver Sun* in the 1950s. They were a boisterous band whose voices and laughter have echoed through the second half of the century. Wherever there were stories to be told they were on the scene, striving to be first with the facts. Each day there were pages to be filled, and each edition was a challenge. Each interview was met with fairness, excitement, and pride, and this epitomized their approach to news gathering. The Mulligan Affair was one of the great stories of their time.

Acknowledgments

We wish to express our thanks to the following, who provided information and assistance in digging out pertinent information about the Mulligan Affair:

Jack Webster, reporter and broadcaster
Charlie King, Ottawa, retired journalist
John King, Toronto, *Globe and Mail*
Kaye Fulton, Ottawa, journalist
Hon. H.A.D. Oliver, QC
Hon. Stewart McMorran, QC (see below)
Former Attorney General Hon. Robert Bonner, QC
Janice Williams, Vancouver Police Department
Debbie Millward, Pacific Press Library
Donna Jean McKinnon, Vancouver Archives
Sharon Shipley, National Library, Ottawa
Vera Lucas, Victoria research

The Scrapbook

While researching this story the authors arranged to interview retired judge and former city prosecutor Stewart McMorran. During the meeting Mr. McMorran unveiled a grand relic of another era—his hand-tailored, 24x30-inch scrapbook of news clippings on the Mulligan Inquiry. With most sources now limited to microfiche, this collection of weathered hard-copy headlines, photos, and articles yielded a unique illustration of the impact the inquiry had on Vancouver. Photo collages used to illustrate the story have been derived from this collection.

Clippings and photographs not otherwise credited (see page 160) have been reproduced with the acknowledgement of the *Vancouver Sun* and *Vancouver Province*. Their support and the assistance of numerous staff has been appreciated. This book contains the work of the following photographers: Harry Filion, Brian Kent, Bill Dennett, and Henry Tregillas of the *Vancouver Sun*; and Eric Cable, Gordon Sedawie, and Bill Cunningham of the *Vancouver Province*.

Table of Contents

Dedication 3

Acknowledgments 4

Leading Players 6

Foreword 9

Prologue: Squad Room Despair 11

1. Mulligan's Vancouver 17

2. The Police Department 24

3. Mulligan, the Man 33

4. Mulligan Battles Crime Wave 37

5. The Reporters 42

6. The Probe Begins 57

7. Crowds Gather—July 13 63

8. Cuthbert Testifies 77

9. Popular Policeman Dies 89

10. Norris vs The Union 92

11. Femme Fatale 97

12. Norris Battles Back 101

13. The Veiled Lady's Ordeal 105

14. Commissioners and Politicians 109

15. Mulligan Makes His Move 115

16. The Final Days 124

17. Mulligan Nailed 129

18. Sunny California 135

19. In Retrospect—40 Years Later 138

     Judge H.A.D. Oliver 140

     Judge Stewart McMorran 143

     Honorable Robert Bonner 146

     Jack Webster 149

20. Winners and Losers.. 151

21. Different Days, Different Cops 155

Credits 160

Leading Players
in the 1955/6 Mulligan Affair

The Inquiry Commission:
Reginald H. Tupper, QC, Commissioner
J.G.A. Hutcheson, QC, Chief Counsel
Victor Dryer, Assistant Counsel

Vancouver Police Commission:
Gerry McGeer, Mayor, 1946-47, Chairman
Charles Thompson, Mayor, 1948-50, Chairman
Fred Hume, Mayor, 1951-58, Chairman
Magistrate Oscar Orr, 1940s-56
Judge Rey Sargent, 1940s-56

Police Department Hierarchy June 1, 1955:
Walter Mulligan, Chief
Gordon Ambrose, Deputy Chief
Alan Rossiter, Traffic Superintendent and Acting Chief during
    Mulligan's suspension
Harry Whelan, Uniform Division Superintendent
Jack Horton, Criminal Investigation Branch Superintendent (CIB)
Pete Lamont, Inspector, gambling
Archie Plummer, Detective Sergeant, gambling, drugs
Len Cuthbert, Detective Sergeant, gambling
Bob Leatherdale, Detective Sergeant
George Kitson, Detective, gambling
George Archer, Chief, appointed 1956

The Journalists:
Dan Ekman, *Vancouver Province*
Bill Forst, *Vancouver Province*
Himie Koshevoy, *News Herald, Vancouver Province*
    and *Vancouver Sun*
Eddie Moyer, *Vancouver Province*
Ray Munro, *Flash*
Jim Smith, *Vancouver Herald*
Hal Straight, *Vancouver Sun*
Jack Wasserman, *Vancouver Sun*
Jack Webster, Radio CJOR

City Prosecutors:

Stewart McMorran, City Prosecutor, Vancouver, BC
Gordon Scott, Judge, former City Prosecutor

Key Lawyers Heard During Inquiry:

H.A.D. Oliver, Counsel for Cuthbert
Tom Norris, First Counsel for Mulligan
Jay Gould, Second Counsel for Mulligan
Neil Fleishman, Counsel for Munro
Lyle Jestley, Counsel for Horton
Angelo Branca, Counsel for Celona and others
W. W. Lefeaux, Counsel for Douglas
Nicholas Mussallem, Counsel for Mulligan's Nephew

Other Lawyers:

Senator J.W. deB. Farris, QC
Leon Ladner
George L. Murray

Key Witnesses:

Nick Badick, petty crook
Leo Bancroft, bookie
Joe Celona, bookie, bootlegger
Mrs. Mugs Corning, bookie's widow
Helen Elizabeth Douglas, the veiled lady
Norma Moore, Celona's ex-commonlaw wife
T.G. Parsloe, ex-Mountie, secret investigator
Bruce Snider, bookie
George Sutherland, bookie
Pete Wallace, bookie
Jack Whelan, ex-cop, Munro informant
Gordon Wismer, former attorney general

Other Players and Observers:

Hon. Robert Bonner, Attorney General, British Columbia
Jack Price, Member of the Legislative Assembly (MLA)
Lou Ruby, Publisher of *Flash*
Bill Couper, Quadra Club operator

Jack Webster (here holding son Jack in 1953) joined the
Vancouver Sun *in September 1947, only eight months after*
Walter Mulligan (below) became Vancouver's controversial
police chief. Neither man was known much for coddling babies.

Foreword

Walter Mulligan had everything going for him when he became Vancouver's police chief in the late 1940s.

It was a turbulent time for the city, however, and as Vancouver moved into the 1950s crime and the drug problem were on the increase. The police department had not been performing well; its staff was untrained, poorly paid, and riddled with graft and corruption.

Mulligan promised to sweep the place clean, from the administration on down. He was tough, confident, ambitious, and backed by friends in high places.

A complex man, Mulligan was, unfortunately, also a crook. Within two years of moving to the top-cop job, he had roped in a compliant detective sergeant in charge of the gambling squad as his partner-in-crime to rake in protection money from city bookies. Nothing showed on the surface, but he had another life, a girlfriend and a house in the country.

I knew him as a reporter, and I couldn't explain then, or even now, why he threw away the promise of becoming one of Vancouver's great police chiefs.

I made my name in Vancouver as a radio reporter covering the seven-month-long Royal Commission that became known as the Mulligan Affair. For hundreds of hours I read my shorthand account of the startling evidence. The tentacles ran deep into Vancouver and Victoria. In the end the inquiry was a whitewash and Mulligan fled to the States to avoid taking the stand. Nobody ever went to jail.

As a newspaper man, the Mulligan probe introduced me to the world of broadcasting on radio and television, and to the hundreds of thousands of listeners and viewers I got to know over the years. It boosted a career that has been very good to me.

Jack Webster

Prologue
Squad Room Despair

The general public, caught up in this master spellbinder's oratory and broad beaming smile have been labouring under the delusion that honesty was the byword of local law.

Flash, June 1955

Detective Sergeant Len Cuthbert sat slumped in a chair in a bare, drab room, his sunken eyes and drawn face testimony to his personal agony and the tension of the last few days. He was deaf to the sounds of early morning traffic that filtered into Vancouver's Main Street police station. Cuthbert's troubled mind was focused on escaping a world that was crumbling around him and on foregoing a future overshadowed by shame, disgrace, humiliation, and possibly jail.

A dutiful policeman who had followed orders for 30 years, he had been unmasked as a cop on the take, snared in graft and corruption—the receiver in seedy street transactions of paper bags full of money from bookies buying protection. *Flash,* a tabloid scandal sheet, had just blown the whistle on Cuthbert and his boss, Police Chief Walter Mulligan. Its pages revealed rampant corruption in Vancouver's police department. Len Cuthbert knew the *Flash* story was tragically true, and there were others who knew he was deeply involved. It was too late for remorse, too late for hopes of forgiveness.

At 8.15 a.m., June 24, 1955, a warm sunny day, Len Cuthbert pressed the .38 revolver he clutched in his hand to his chest and squeezed the trigger. A bullet tore through his body and slammed into the wall behind him. Somehow he missed his heart. The shot brought colleagues rushing into the

Walter Mulligan, seen here in the annual PNE parade, rode tall in the saddle longer than any other Vancouver police chief before him.

room where he sat, conscious but in shock, mumbling apologies that he hadn't died. Len Cuthbert failed in his attempted suicide as he had failed in his life.

In the coming months, Cuthbert would face the living hell he had tried to escape, as the most sweeping public inquiry in Vancouver police history tore apart his character, his life, and the lives of many others who worked in the department. His gunshot triggered a crisis few Vancouverites could have imagined. Newspaper stories about a badly flawed police force were common, but no one had taken them seriously. Few at this stage believed high-ranking officers could be involved. They did not know that Cuthbert's partner in crime was his boss, Police Chief Walter Mulligan.

Big, assertive, confident, well-connected Walter Mulligan had been police chief since 1947. Embraced by many politicians and civic leaders, he was not well respected within the police force itself. *Flash* and its local reporter Ray Munro asserted that, since Mulligan leapfrogged to the top job "over the objections of more than half the force, the general public, caught up in this master spellbinder's oratory and broad beaming smile have been labouring under the delusion that honesty was the byword of local law. Hah!"

The echo of Len Cuthbert's gunshot brought the force into the limelight, and the sound had barely died away when Attorney General Robert Bonner ordered an inquiry that would tear the veneer from Vancouver's law-and-order enforcers and reveal great breaches in a police department riddled with rot. Up to this time, Vancouver had had a fascinating relationship with its police force. A half-century of questionable antics, stop-gap solutions, and some underhanded dealings had established a number of peculiar precedents. Then came Mulligan, a student of the system.

From mid-1955 through to spring 1956, most of Canada and parts of the United States were caught up in the drama of Vancouver's Tupper Inquiry into the activities of Mulligan and the Vancouver Police Department. Fist fights broke out as hundreds pushed and shoved to get a seat in the court house in order to see the saga unfold. Media coverage was massive. The inquiry had everything reporters wanted: graft, corruption, death, bootleggers, bookies, vice-lords, politicians with a sudden loss of memory, gambling squad cops who could barely remember their names, hookers, and Mulligan's own black-veiled "mystery" lady. Canadian newspapers proclaimed it the news story of the year.

* * *

The Mulligan probe had barely begun when another Vancouver policeman fired a bullet into his chest. Superintendent Harry Whelan's suicide rocked the commission. Head of the Uniform Division, described as an honest, clean cop, he had been distraught for some time. He knew Mulligan was on the take and feared his own brother Jack was involved. Called to testify before the commission, Whelan was willing to expose Mulligan, whom he and many others disliked, but he faced a greater problem. A brash young lawyer warned Whelan the day before his demise to expect stiff cross-examination from Mulligan's legal defence team. The superintendent was afraid he would be forced to reveal several sad facts about his personal life that would embarrass his family. Whelan was the inquiry's great casualty, and he left behind a widow and two young sons.

A media frenzy was generated by the inquiry. Vancouver dailies, nervous about the laws of libel and the involvement of various community leaders in alleged illegal activity, had been amassing information for months but had failed to print any of it. The *Vancouver Sun*, the *Vancouver Province,* and the *Vancouver Herald* now jumped into the fray, printing and photographing everything they could dig up. Gargantuan headlines became commonplace. Wire services picked up the stories and fed them across the country and across the continent.

The two major dailies, in particular the *Vancouver Province*, had the opportunity to run the story before *Flash* but lacked the guts to do so. Throughout the inquiry the two papers' publishers were constantly reminded of their sad initial performances. The jibes came from a new radio voice, a former *Sun* man turned broadcaster who went on air nightly for up to five hours at a stretch and read his blow-by-blow shorthand notes of the testimony. Ratings soared for radio station CJOR as thousands sat with their ears glued to their sets, deciphering every word spoken by the immigrant Scot. For Jack Webster, the newsman with the sounds of Glasgow etched permanently in his throat, the Mulligan Affair was a launching pad to fame and fortune.

The legal profession embraced the proceedings with zest. Some of Vancouver's high-powered, high-priced lawyers were assured hefty fees. The court house filled with their rhetoric, their fiery debate, and their clashes with the inquiry commissioner. There were charges from one leading attorney that there had been attempts to blackmail him.

The Tupper Inquiry became the most sweeping probe of the Vancouver Police Department ever held. Prior investigations had relieved former chiefs of their responsibilities or fulfilled a politician's need for a scapegoat, but nobody dug deep. Mulligan's became the first inquiry to reach well beneath the surface. While it answered some questions about police corruption, the inquiry gained its notoriety because it left so many others unasked and unanswered, encouraging the rumour mill to function at top speed. The most notable omissions related to the three-man Police Commission. These civic leaders, who were responsible for the performance of the force, had heard the allegations against Mulligan many times and had ignored them. Since 1949 they had sat on information that suggested Mulligan was accepting bribes. At the inquiry their explanations for this were often confused, contradictory, and vague, leaving reporters and the public filled with wonder and more than a little suspicion.

After the devastating *Flash* exposé the Police Commission hurriedly called a closed-door meeting that went on for hours. At its conclusion, Attorney General Robert Bonner was asked to initiate a Royal Commission of Inquiry into Mulligan's police force. Bonner chose Reginald H. Tupper, QC, a 62-year-old former head of the Faculty of Law at the University of British Columbia, to head the probe.

The startling evidence that emerged in the early days of the inquiry soon prompted Bonner to name a special RCMP squad to investigate statements and charges arising from the welter of evidence and conflicting testimony. The Mounties' work caused a series of delays during the seven months the proceedings held centre stage in the province. In all, the inquiry sat for 40 days, heard 126 witnesses, catalogued 144 exhibits, and obtained information from 300 people who were questioned. It cost taxpayers $57,000 plus change—a bargain at today's prices.

Despite far-reaching sleuthing by both media and special investigators, the Mulligan Affair was famous more for its secrets than for its disclosures. The full story was never told, and now it is too late to ask some of the important questions because many of the leading characters have left the stage. Still, enough of the key players remain to reconstruct, to analyze, and to discuss what happened in Vancouver during the Mulligan Affair, one of the biggest scandals of the 1950s.

On June 24, 1955, with the morning suicide attempt of Len Cuthbert, the Vancouver dailies took off the gloves and jumped on a story many reporters had long sought to break. In its three-star final edition the Vancouver Province *used 4½-inch headlines to shout CITY DETECTIVE SHOOTS HIMSELF. Likewise the* Vancouver Sun, *in its afternoon edition, broke the Mulligan story using photographer Bill Dennett's graphic photo of Cuthbert being hauled through the mirrored police station entrance to a waiting ambulance. The Dennett lens also found a content Ray Munro and so-called bodyguard Jack Whelan reading the startling story in the morning edition of the* Sun, *only 24 hours after Chief Mulligan had sued Munro for libel. The 5-star final held the dramatic photo, but a new headline reported the latest speculation.*

tective Fails in Suicide Bid

OUNTIE REPORTED
O REPLACE CHIEF

The Vancouver Sun **FINAL EDITION** ★★★★

Discussion Confirmed

WOUNDED OFFICER RUSHED TO HOSPITAL

The Vancouver Sun

Detective Shoots Self, Mulligan Reported Out in Police Crisis

Mountie Likely To Take Over

Suicide Attempted In Police Station

'I'm Sorry I Missed My Heart'

WOUNDED OFFICER RUSHED TO HOSPITAL

Could Have Him 2 Years

Followed Libel Suit

According to 'Blue Book'

City Police Hop From Crisis To Crisis in Turbulent Year

Death 'Only Way,' Cuthbert Told Sun

CITY DETECTIVE
SHOOTS HIMSELF

The Vancouver Province
A Dependable Newspaper

Cuthbert wounded at police station

Meetings on police

Ex-gambling squad head near death

This 1955/56 photo (top left) of Vancouver's city centre captures a city on the brink of change. The Hotel Vancouver, next to the hidden court house, and Marine Building (far right) dominate the skyline. Behind the hotel, near Hornby and Robson, derelict homes (bottom left) were being dismantled to make way for 777 Hornby, a highrise home to many Vancouver lawyers, including H.A.D. Oliver. Georgia and Granville (upper right) was the commercial hub, with its famous Birks Clock and diagonal crosswalks. In the background the Georgia and Devonshire Hotels, across from the court house, were the favoured places of respite during the Tupper Inquiry.

I. Mulligan's Vancouver

Gambling and prostitution supplied the funds which made it possible to corrupt law enforcers.

Angelo Branca

In 1955 Vancouver was a youthful, lively city growing up fast, but it was not an easy time for the police department because crime was on the upsurge and the top cop was a crook. In the United States Prohibition produced the "roaring twenties." Western Canada roared later. In British Columbia, antiquated legislation, population growth, and Vancouver's location at the end of the line for anyone heading west came together to produce an era that can best be described as the "roaring" rather than the "fabulous" fifties. This was Walter Mulligan's world.

There had been a steady build-up to this era, a reaction to the end of the Second World War. This build-up involved a loosening of tensions and restrictions, an influx of new people and new money, changes in social values, and a sense of exuberant extravagance. The price paid was a breakdown in law and order. Bootlegging was rampant, and liquor consumption had become a problem. Any cab delivered a $4.50 bottle of rye for $6. News stands and smoke shops were bookie outlets. Hookers openly plied the streets, operating out of hotels and rooming houses. Drugs began to take a heavy toll.

By the late 1940s, *Vancouver Sun* managing editor Hal Straight knew the police department was graft-ridden. Tips picked up on the street by reporters continuously fuelled his suspicions about some members of the force and its new chief, Walter Mulligan, who had been appointed in 1947. Jack Webster, at this time a *Sun* reporter, was assigned to investigate and wound up living in skid row's scabrous hotels for two weeks. While organized crime was minor league by New York or Chicago standards, Webster found a lot of rot in Vancouver's underpinnings. Authorities were aware of gambling and vice, but as long as it was confined to a small area next to Chinatown they preferred to ignore it. Now the *Sun* announced it was spreading.

According to Webster's skid-row exposé:

> *Hundreds of professional gamblers operate in the city, many of them taking part in illegal games—mostly poker—which take place after hours in city clubs, in phony sports clubs and plain illegal joints ... Bookmakers, their employees, touts and runners, operate in beer parlours, cigar stores, hotel lounges, taxi offices and what amounts to open "betting halls" ... Bootleggers, free from competition from any all-night liquor stores, supply liquor freely on telephone orders, sell it to personal callers and even dish it out by the glass in private "lounges."*

Webster found police acting as doormen at bookie joints, and nothing disappeared faster than a speeding ticket when a bottle of booze was delivered quickly to the cop who wrote it. Not all were on the take, just a lot of them. Conditions hadn't improved when Walter Mulligan's reign moved into the 1950s. The *Sun* demanded that there be an official investigation and kept hammering away at the issue, but all its efforts were ignored.

Angelo Branca, a colourful criminal lawyer who maintained his office in the east end, knew the situation well and agreed with Webster's findings. He defended many well known criminals before becoming a respected BC Appeal Court judge. In his memoirs he wrote: "Gambling and prostitution supplied the funds which made it possible to corrupt law enforcers. Betting was widespread. In 1951, after 565 convictions in six years against betting shops in Vancouver, the trade was flourishing as never before. If bribing policemen and city politicians did not keep them out of court, the bookmakers hired the best lawyers in town to keep them out of jail."

Vancouver, still very much a young urban upstart, was yet to blossom into a vibrant city. Streetcars rattled across the old Granville Street Bridge until 1954. Then a new bridge, built without tracks, opened, and trolley buses appeared for the first time. The city was still small enough that most people who went downtown for a night out met under the Birks clock at Georgia and Granville before heading to the movies.

Vancouver, still vying with Winnipeg for recognition as Canada's third largest city (after Montreal and Toronto), was almost unknown in the capitals of Europe or the teeming cities of Asia. Those who had found it, about 400,000, believed they were living in one of the best places in the world. They had magnificent scenery, a high standard of living, clean beaches for summer swimming, skiing on the North Shore mountains (providing you didn't mind the hike to get there), and the best climate in the country, rain notwithstanding.

Thanks to the fire of 1886, which gutted the early city, nothing much was over 50 years old. Comfortable wooden houses with broad porches and tidy gardens still crowded the West End. The Sylvia Hotel advertised its eight-storey-high dining room, where you could "dine in the sky high above English Bay." Low-rise buildings were common in the downtown area. Dominating the skyline were the multi-storied Marine Building, the new Vancouver Hotel, and the Medical-Dental Building on Georgia across from the court house. The Vancouver Block on Granville and the Rogers Building were still prestigious addresses. Farther east was the Sun Tower and the city's oldest high-rise, the red-domed bank at Victory Square, kitty-corner to the home of the *Province*.

Further along Pender Street Chinatown had been an intrinsic part of Vancouver since the Chinese arrived in the 1880s to help build the Canadian Pacific Railway. By the 1950s many Asians still resided in the area, although a new generation was moving to the suburbs and integrating into the larger community. Many of the elders stuck to the security of their traditional ways and lived in narrow three- or four-storey buildings decorated with pagoda-like roofs and tiny balconies. These early immigrants remembered Vancouver's race riots and felt safer in their own neighbourhood. On a warm day the clink of tiles could be heard, as old men played Mah Jong or Fan Tan in upstairs rooms. Walter Mulligan and his men knew the area well, as did drug dealers, bookies, and gamblers; but few other Vancouverites ventured much beyond their favourite Chinese restaurant.

Vancouver's youth, who had grown up knowing nothing but war, were finding their feet. For most of them these were good times, and generally there was a job for anyone who wanted to work. The University of British Columbia (UBC) had exploded into life. Returned servicemen living on educational allowances mixed with fresh young "bobby soxers" who had grown up listening to nightly war news on the radio but had escaped the actual horrors of the conflict. Working women were the norm during the war years, but a girl graduating from high school still often went to UBC to search for a "husband with prospects." With ten men for every woman on campus, it was a good place to look.

Businesses thrived and expanded to feed public demands for new consumer goods. Beyond the Lower Mainland lay endless forests, well-stocked salmon streams, and precious metals waiting to be found. The people of Vancouver were rushing to an unimagined future, impatient to be getting on with it. They found the strict laws and regulations that had been imposed in the 1930s and during the war years difficult to live with. For example, drinking in restaurants or other "public places" was prohibited. Such ludicrous regulations resulted in a general disrespect for the law. In the 1950s it was common to see well-dressed partygoers out for a night on the town carrying a brown paper bag. They would smuggle a bottle, probably of rye or rum, into a cabaret where, after paying a cover charge, they would be supplied with mixer and ice at outrageous prices. Public nightclubs were not allowed to sell or serve liquor. Walter Mulligan's liquor squad paid regular visits to most of them, but a customer had to admit ownership of a bottle before a charge could be laid. Bottles were kept under the table, and when police arrived everyone would be on the dance floor and have no idea who owned what. It was a silly charade.

Vancouver's social life was reported daily in the "Women's Pages" of the newspapers, but there was no mention of the brown bags carried by men decked out in tuxedos escorting fashionable women in long velvet gowns. Gossip columnists described each evening's events in detail and included long lists of attendees. The winter season was highlighted by the "Debutante's Ball" at HMCS *Discovery* in Stanley Park. College beauties reigned as "Queen of the Mardi Gras" or the "Sweetheart of Sigma Chi." From the ranks of the city's newsrooms men and women donned their finest once a year to attend the Press Ball at the Commodore Cabaret. Booze flowed freely, while dancer's enjoyed the famous spring-loaded floor. This was followed by the Policemens' Ball at the same venue, attended annually by Chief Walter Mulligan. In a more intimate atmosphere atop the Hotel Vancouver, young sophisticates danced to the music of Dal Richards at the Roof, which was not raided as often as was the Commodore Ballroom.

The situation was complicated for both residents and for Mulligan's police force. There were dozens of so-called private drinking clubs that were not legally defined as "public places." These included legions, working men's clubs, and watering holes having vague ethnic requirements for membership. At the Arctic Club members could buy a drink and listen to the piano stylings of Chris Gage. The young and the restless also dropped in to the PA (Pacific Athletic) Club, the Quadra Club, or even the Penthouse (a favourite hooker hangout).

Even beer parlours selling seven-ounce suds for 10 cents were saddled with restrictive regulations and forced by law to paint their windows black or dark brown so passers-by would not see the sin and degradation going on inside. Another peculiarity of the time was that pubs were segregated into "Mens" and "Ladies and Escorts" sections, each with a separate entrance.

The laws were archaic, confusing, and often inconsistent: as a result, they were often ignored. At the more expensive night spots there was an intermingling of the good, the bad, the influential, and the merely monied, all of whom liked to be seen at places like the Cave Supper Club, Isy's, the Palomar, or the W.K and Mandarin Gardens in Chinatown. All of these establishments seemed capable of making sure their respective clienteles got what they wanted. Elsewhere, the down-and-outs drank 90-cent wine under the city's bridges or along the scummy banks of False Creek. Their empties were strewn amid the machine shops and abandoned broken-down sheds.

Along Main Street, the fire hall and coroner's office sat next to the old police station. The city prosecutor's office was housed on the upper floor above the active police station pictured here.

In the 1950s, racism in Vancouver was ignored if not condoned. Walter Koerner, a pre-war Jewish refugee, escaped with his wife from Nazi-occupied Czechoslovakia in 1939. He prospered in business in Vancouver and, in 1955, donated a million dollars to education, charity, and culture. This lumber magnate, however, could not have joined the Vancouver Club had he wanted to because it didn't admit Jews or Asians. Women were allowed on the premises only when escorted by a member and only during certain hours. They entered by the side door and could go only to designated areas, a practice that continued until the 1990s.

In 1955 "political correctness" was an unknown phrase. The popular humour of the day designated the Smiling Buddha nightspot as the Chuckling Chink and dubbed an area where some East Indians lived as the Khyber Pass. It was a time when Liberal immigration minister Jack Pickersgill could state, when visiting Vancouver: "If equally good people, the Canadian baby is better than an immigrant as an addition to the population of Canada." He also opined that newcomers from Great Britain and the countries of northern and western Europe, "whose historical traditions and political and social views are more like our own," fit in better than did others. Most agreed with him.

In Mulligan's Vancouver success in business or trade was epitomized by owning a home on the west side—Kitsilano, Kerrisdale, Dunbar, or Point Grey. On the east side were the older established neighbourhoods of Fairview and Mount Pleasant. There was also an area of Strathcona known as the "Mile of Vice." Unknown and largely unseen by young families carving out a niche for themselves, it was frequented by many well-heeled men—from politicians to bookies, from policemen to newsmen and loggers with fat wallets. Any woman walking the Mile was assumed to be working.

In the 1950s the city and its surrounding suburbs were expanding rapidly, and experts predicted the population would reach a million by the year 2000. They were only out by a million or so. The new arrivals provided new ideas and, sometimes, cheap labour. In the early 1950s the most recent influx of immigrants came from Great Britain. These people were well represented within the business community, within the police force, and within the dailies, which, in conjunction with radio, carried the news of the day. Black-and-white TV was in its infancy.

Since the 1920s, British Columbia had been controlled by the provincial Liberal party. To head off growing public discontent and the increasing popularity of the Left-wing Cooperative Commonwealth Federation (CCF), the Liberals joined with the Tories and formed a Coalition Party headed by Liberal premier Byron Ingemar ("Boss Johnson") and his flamboyant attorney general Gordon Wismer. There were many tales of Wismer's adventures, as he was sometimes escorted by Walter Mulligan's finest to various "after-hours" clubs. Wismer was welcome in all of them. He was cheerful and a free spender—qualities that endeared him to club owners. As attorney general, on at least two occasions he refused requests from the Police Commission to order an inquiry into the activities of Mulligan's police department. Wismer claimed there was insufficient evidence to do so. Local media were among those who felt that, on the contrary, there was plenty of evidence. Their suspicions were aroused because not only had they seen the attorney general associating with Vancouver's known criminal element, but they also knew he was a buddy of Mulligan.

By 1952 the Liberal-Conservative Coalition was history as the new Social Credit government, under W.A.C. ("Wacky") Bennett, took control of provincial politics. Supported by a constituency of the church-going public, abstainers, and grass-roots fundamentalists, the new Right-wing government brought about many changes. Bennett vowed to open up the province to business, and the slow, overnight boat to Vancouver Island gave way to the faster BC Ferry Service. New highways began to snake their way through the Interior of the province under highways minister and church pastor "Flying" Phil Gaglardi. It was, however, a number of years before the Socred's risked the wrath of the church by relaxing the old liquor laws to bring an end to the brown bags that cluttered the floors of Vancouver's hotels and ballrooms.

In March 1955, the *Province* and the *Sun* raised their price to seven cents from five. Meanwhile, regulators refused permission for the BC Electric Company to raise the price of bus fares from 13 to 15 cents, and there was public opposition to hiking parking metres to 10 cents an hour. The cost of building the proposed Second Narrows Bridge was estimated at $11 million.

The BC Lions celebrated their first birthday in the new Empire Stadium, the venue for the 1954 British Empire Games and the dramatic sub-four-minute mile run by Roger Bannister and John Landy.

In 1955, at least one Vancouver policeman sang a song that Walter Mulligan liked. In April Constable Harry Petria won the operatic solo class for men at the BC Music Festival. At the same time Reverend Stanley Higgs of St Michael's Anglican Church was flooded with calls meant for a bootlegger with a similar phone number. He asked parishioners to flood the bootlegger with calls in the hope of getting him either to see the light or to change his number. Stanley Park was 67 years old, and, in June, Theatre Under the Stars was rained out for the opening night of *Anything Goes*. The musical's title aptly portrayed Vancouver's atmosphere.

Only a few officials and the odd investigative reporter had any reservations about members of the police force who pounded a beat in their neighbourhoods or took care of traffic problems. Chief Mulligan was much in demand as a speaker at churches and mens' clubs.

The day after Len Cuthbert was wheeled out of the police station on a gurney, even the most blasé Vancouverite was surprised by the charges and counter-charges. In the ensuing weeks and months newspaper headlines and radio news bulletins revealed the depth and breadth of gambling, book-making, crime, and corruption that were rampant in the city. Such goings on could be found, not only in all the smoke shops on the east side, but also beneath the fedoras at Milo the Hatter's, an upscale bookie joint on West Pender.

Suddenly everybody wanted to know a lot more about Chief Walter Mulligan and the Vancouver Police Department.

2.   The Police Department

In true Hollywood style the gangsters smashed out the rear
window of their car and proceeded to shoot at the pursuing
police car with shotguns and revolvers.

A Vancouver newspaper

The history of Vancouver's police department is as colourful as is that of the community it represents. It has had conscientious, capable performers, men who gave their lives to protect the citizenry, as well as some bad apples. The members of the force have worn everything from Keystone Kop uniforms to English Bobby take-offs, and they have frequently suffered from political interference and lack of direction. Almost a century after its origins, the force would suffer from the ambitions of Walter Mulligan.

The first police department was established in 1859, when Gastown was barely a community. An Irishman named Charlie Brew was appointed Inspector of Police by James Douglas, Governor and Commander-in-Chief of Her Majesty's Colony of British Columbia. He maintained that the criminal and civil laws of England would be enforced. The lawmen started out as a rag-tag band with a lot of muscle and not much else. Brew, who eventually had a force of 15, built the first log jailhouse near Gassy Jack's Saloon. A few years later, according to the official history of the Vancouver Police Department, one settler wrote in his diary: "Mr. Brew and a few others called looking for a murderer." The following day, he wrote: "Mr. Brew and Co. called and ate breakfast." Whether they captured the killer or just some ham and eggs is unknown. Brew was replaced in 1871 when, in a petition, he was accused of having trouble handling drunks and violence.

Today tourists roam a restored Gastown where Gassy Jack Deighton opened one of the first saloons. Times turned sour for his establishment and Gassy Jack went broke. When he died in 1875 it was top cop Jonathan Miller, successor to Mr. Brew, who provided the suit in which Deighton was buried.

Vancouver officially became a city in 1886 and, within a year, John Stewart, the first police chief, reported that drug use was spreading beyond the Chinese community. Early Vancouver regulations allowed opium

In 1886, shortly after Vancouver's great fire, Brew & Company stand ready to keep the peace. Chartres "Charlie" Brew had a long career in BC policing. His success rate was summed up in the words of historian H.H. Bancroft: "Never in the pacification and settlement of any section of America has there been so few disturbances, so few crimes against law and order."

manufacture, providing an annual $500 fee was paid. Although the dens were soon outlawed, the public retained the view that the drug trade was centred in Chinatown. Chief Stewart said that there were 50 White users in the city "who were beyond redemption."

The Chinese had long faced discrimination. Both their industry and their opium dens made many people nervous. This type of reasoning was prevalent in early Vancouver and, in 1887, prompted the Knights of Labour to begin campaigning against Chinese immigration. The Anti-Chinese League followed and, later, was supplanted by the Asiatic Exclusion League, which also promulgated an aversion to the Japanese community. Disturbances lasted for 20 years, and policing in Vancouver often focused on the differences between "ethnic" communities. There were frequent beatings as well as knife and club fights. Black crosses were painted on buildings where Asians worked. In 1907 the federal government paid the Chinese $20,000 and the Japanese $9,000, respectively, for property damage. At the time the Asian population was about 10 percent of the city total of 65,000.

The jobs of men in the Vancouver police force were complicated by the character of the city itself—a coastal community at the end of the line that attracted more than its share of dodgers and drifters. Because Vancouver was well known as a lusty spot, in 1907 it received an influx of hookers from

San Francisco when an earthquake put a crimp in business in California. From across the Pacific the perennial flow of drugs continued.

Malcolm MacLellan, who became chief in 1913, worried about the impact of narcotics on his city and took a more progressive view than was generally held at that time. The Vancouver Police Department's official history states: "He lobbied for drug users to be treated as human beings in need of medical help rather than as criminals, but called for stiffer penalties for persons convicted of selling illegal drugs. His pleas fell on deaf ears." It was both tragic and ironic that he was gunned down during the arrest of a man addicted to morphine and cocaine. MacLellan was a take-charge chief, who elected to lead the assault on the apartment where the suspect was hiding. He died leading the charge. The killer, Bob Tait, committed suicide on the spot.

The police union that Walter Mulligan would battle throughout his tenure as chief was formed in 1918, as constables banded together in order to demand better wages and working conditions. Their first win was a guaranteed one day off a week.

Walter Mulligan joined the department on April 21, 1927, and began pounding a beat on Broadway between Granville and Main. It was a year marked by a vice probe that ended with Mayor Louis Taylor being accused of obtaining campaign funds from gambling king Shu Moy and meeting socially with Joe Celona, an owner of bawdyhouses.

The Great Depression brought new problems. Colonel W.W. Foster was hired as chief in 1935. He had no police experience but had won the Distinguished Service Order and two bars in the First World War. One of his first acts was to enforce the Riot Act read by Mayor Gerry McGeer, when thousands of the unemployed attended a mass rally demanding jobs. When the many who travelled to BC seeking work couldn't find it in Vancouver, the scene at Victory Square turned ugly.

In his time, Gerry McGeer was one of Vancouver's most flamboyant characters. As a lawyer who worked the police courts, he became acquainted with Walter Mulligan. Entering politics he served as a Liberal Member of the Legislative Assembly (MLA) in Victoria but, in 1935, entered civic politics and became mayor of Vancouver for a two-year term. Another switch took him to Ottawa, where he served as a Member of Parliament (MP) for eight years. Nominated to the Senate in 1946, he again ran for Mayor of Vancouver and won the election handily.

Meanwhile, by the mid-1930s, Mulligan had advanced from pounding a beat to riding a motor bike as a traffic officer. Most of the department and the public was impressed by Chief Foster's fix-bayonets-and-charge style, which captured newspaper headlines. Mulligan wasn't in on the chase, but it was the talk of the station when Foster pursued the "Silk Stocking Gang," the members of which disguised themselves with stocking masks. Another of

Foster's newspaper episodes concerned the "Blue Sedan Bandits" who, with a certain élan, stole only blue vehicles.

Foster clearly imprinted his leadership on the department and gained the respect of his men. He was riding in a squad car one night when he saw what appeared to be a stolen vehicle and gave chase through city streets. As reported by newspapers of the day: "In true Hollywood style the gangsters smashed out the rear window of their car and proceeded to shoot at the pursuing police car with shotguns and revolvers."

The chief and his driver charged on. Their car was "riddled with shots, the radiator punctured and leaking, the windshield shattered, and the whole front end peppered with shotgun pellets." The fleeing mobsters eventually piled up their car and fled from the wreck, still wearing masks and carrying guns. Foster's driver fired and dropped one man, who subsequently provided the names of his three companions, two of whom were later captured. For the sanguine Foster, it was just another day in the trenches. He received a written commendation from city council (his driver seemed to get the better

A former colonel, W.W. Foster kept a lid on the city during the late 30s, including the Post Office riot of 1938.

deal—an engraved gold watch). The old soldier quit the force to go back to war in 1940 and did not return to the department.

Throughout its history the police department was fortunate to have men like MacLellan, Foster, and Robert McBeath. The latter was a Scotsman who joined the army at age 16 and won the Victoria Cross at Cambray, only to die a few years later at Granville and Davie when gunned down by a motorist he had stopped on suspicion of drunk driving. While it had its heroes, the department also had its share of chiefs, officers, and beat pounders who were fired for various forms of graft and corruption.

In one famous probe early in the century, it was found that the chief, the city prosecutor, the city auditor, and one cop were splitting money from various payoffs. They were all fired, but the chief and prosecutor were later rehired.

The most sweeping and sensational probe of all was yet to come. It resulted from the rapid advancement of young Walter Mulligan. He was promoted to detective in 1937, 10 years after joining the force. Police records show that he made his first major mark in 1944, following the killing of a man during an armed hold-up attempt at a bootlegging blind pig on Howe Street. "The case was assigned to a young detective named Walter Mulligan," states the history. "His subsequent arrest and charge of two suspects was to do much to enhance his career." It also brought him to the attention of Gerry McGeer, who would soon return as Mayor of Vancouver and become Mulligan's mentor.

In 1945, Alex McNeill, the former deputy chief, began his brief tenure as the top cop. It was bad timing for McNeill. The department was seriously undermanned, awaiting the return of servicemen to fill the gaps. In the meantime there was a dramatic increase in crime. Gangs of "Zoot Suiters" hung out on downtown corners, and violence became a concern.

In an attempt to improve the situation, Chief McNeill reorganized the department, forming a new Criminal Investigation Branch (CIB). To the surprise of many, the superintendent of the new branch was the youngest applicant. Mulligan, who had risen to the rank of sergeant, jumped three full categories to take on the new position in August 1946. Senior applicants in line for the job were more than surprised; their emotions ranged from disappointment to outrage. Many suggested that Mulligan's carefully developed association with Gerry McGeer had paid off.

Mulligan was on his way. With his newfound authority he readily delved into the organization and performance of the vital morality, gambling, and liquor squads, hinting at major changes to come. The rumour mill went into overdrive. Some policemen believed he was only doing what had to be done, convinced a clean sweep was needed. Others felt his drive was too much too soon, powered by overwhelming personal ambition and the will of Mayor Gerry McGeer.

Long time political animal Gerry McGeer backed Mulligan to the hilt in 1947 as he shook up both the department and the police commission during his final days as Vancouver's mayor. Their combined reign would be brief.

The *Province* reported the angry reaction of some members of the force: "The station was buzzing like an angry hornets' nest when the force learned of Mulligan's main demand in taking over the job—that members of these three squads be placed back in uniform." A large and important segment of the force was developing a dislike for Walter Mulligan.

On January 13, 1947, only five months into his new job, Mulligan's manoeuvring paid off in a big way. The *Sun* reported that it took only a seconds-long meeting between Mulligan and the beleaguered Chief McNeill before a major announcement was made. Mulligan would assume responsibility for the morality, gambling, and liquor squads under the CIB.

Backroom manoeuvring continued, and within hours McNeill reneged and announced he was tossing the whole problem of reorganizing the department to the Police Commission. He had been expected to announce that 23 members of the plain clothes squads would be put back into uniform, while specially selected men would be appointed to Mulligan's new unit.

In the ensuing uproar the police commissioner, Magistrate MacKenzie Matheson, quit. Mayor McGeer, who was in hospital for a post-operative check-up, announced that the commissioner had quit for health reasons.

Matheson promptly announced he had never been healthier. His real reasons for quitting were never made fully clear, but insiders said he was unhappy with Mayor McGeer's handling of the police department and the favouritism shown towards Mulligan. Matheson was replaced immediately by Lieutenant-Colonel C.H. Hill, a former assistant commissioner of the RCMP. On January 24, Inspector Walter Bell, who had headed the gambling squad for 10 years, also resigned. Bell had been targetted by Mayor McGeer as a cop who had to go to answer for the fact that bookmaking was running rampant in Vancouver.

Then came a series of surprising announcements some termed a set up. On January 25 Walter Mulligan became acting police chief following an hour-long meeting of the Police Commission, chaired by Gerry McGeer. McNeill was suspended until his scheduled retirement in four months. Also out on their ears were the deputy chief and six other officers. Mulligan's acting role lasted about 48 hours, and, on January 27, he became the youngest police chief in Vancouver's history.

Among the causes for chaos in the police department, McGeer listed poor accommodation in the old cramped headquarters, poor equipment, and the wholly unsuitable superannuation allowances. The mayor said that these factors "contributed to any delinquencies which may have occurred in the past." McNeill was dismissed for "lack of control over his men."

McGeer lauded Mulligan, calling him young, able, courageous, honest, and thoroughly devoted to his duties. The mayor added he was sure Mulligan would have the "unqualified support of all well-meaning members of the force." Not everyone agreed. Critics maintained he was too young, inexperienced, and over-eager. There were predictions he wouldn't last.

City Prosecutor Gordon Scott, a veteran Vancouver barrister, also announced his resignation. Scott went public and stated he disagreed "thoroughly with Mayor McGeer's procedure in handling the police situation." Late the following year he returned to the post of city prosecutor.

A storm of controversy continued to hover over Mulligan and the Police Commission. The new chief told the *Province* in February, only weeks after his appointment, that if Mayor McGeer agreed he would go on the radio and "tell all" of the details concerning the 18 months that led to his appointment as chief. "My knowledge of the vice situation and the unsatisfactory squad system under which we operated with its utter lack of cooperation and coordination with the CIB and lack of supervision generally—was the reason for my attempts in 1946 to bring this problem into the open. I failed in this until Mayor McGeer took office." Right or wrong, this raised more hackles among senior officers, who felt that Mulligan was over-zealous in his condemnations.

This radio broadcast was never made, but Mulligan got his chance in a brief public hearing that a reluctant city council ordered the Police Commission to conduct. It took place in city hall and lasted five days, beginning March 18. The hearing heard demands for the reinstatement of some of those who had been fired or suspended on Mulligan's recommendation.

In his battle with Mayor McGeer and Chief Mulligan, Gordon Scott turned from being prosecutor of, to being public defender for, some of the discharged police. Even before the hearing opened, Scott declared the disciplinary action would have to go to arbitration because it contravened the contract between the Police Commission and the union. At the hearing Scott charged that Mayor McGeer had led Mulligan astray during the investigations into police conduct. In words that were to re-echo, Scott claimed that there had been "wholesale acceptance of hearsay evidence." An ironic twist in this defence of the police union was that much of Scott's fiery closing statement never made it to the official record because the stenographer put down his pen at his 6:00 p.m. quitting time, even though the hearing didn't wrap up until 7:00 p.m. *Province* reporter Jack Steppler summed up the situation with the comment: "Same old play, same old stars concluded the last act. There were Mayor McGeer and former city prosecutor Gordon Scott exchanging their final parries, championing opposing camps."

As often occurred when there were allegations of irregularities, the name of Attorney General Gordon Wismer was introduced. Former detective Ben Coultas, who had been dismissed from the force in the Mulligan shakeup, took the stand in his own defence. A former member of the gambling squad, Coultas claimed responsibility for bringing West Georgia Street resident Massey White into court. Coultas told the hearing: "I had him before the magistrate for distributing information helpful to bookmaking, but Mr. Gordon Wismer got him off."

Mulligan repeated his hard line, stating that there had been inefficiency and neglect of duty. In words that would also come back to haunt him, Mulligan testified: "There was no concerted effort that I can see to reduce gambling. My firm conviction is that these places could not operate without police knowledge and sanction." He stated that 45 bookmaking establishments and card games had been operating.

The arbitration board hearing demanded by Scott was chaired by Brigadeer General Sherwood Lett, later Chief Justice of the Supreme Court of British Columbia. Based on a review of evidence from the original hearing, the board upheld the demotions and suspensions of the policemen. Mulligan and McGeer had won. With the backing of a popular and powerful politician and the support of the courts, Mulligan was firmly in the driver's seat, prepared to solidify his own plans for the department.

3.   Mulligan, the Man

By 1953, things were starting to fall apart for Chief Mulligan. Rumours had begun to circulate that he was too friendly with people involved in illegal gambling and there was major discontent within the department.

Official History of Vancouver Police Department

The new 42-year-old police chief was an Irishman from Liverpool and the youngest chief the city had known. He was the youngest of nine children and the son of a police inspector who emigrated from England to Vancouver in 1919. Walter Mulligan joined the merchant marine in 1922 and spent five years at sea. He would always profess his love for the ocean, although he never owned a boat.

After quitting the merchant marine he applied for a job with the Vancouver Police Department in 1927—a time when size and muscle were still the main prerequisites for being a police officer. He had plenty of both. Broad shouldered, with dark hair and heavy features, he was six-foot-two-inches tall and weighed 230 pounds. His size alone made him a domineering figure; it was a figure that would command law and order in Canada's third largest city and one day would set Vancouver on its heels. He kept his weight under control by going on a bird-like diet. Generally soft spoken, he had a booming voice when the need arose and took pride in his ability to influence or sway an audience. He was confident and ambitious. While he had little formal education, he was an avid reader, favouring historical, travel, and autobiographical books. Gardening was a favourite hobby, and he won prizes in local competitions for his flowers.

Chief Walter Mulligan was both gregarious and visible in his early years as police chief. Always accessible, he is seen here in pipe band garb at the 1949 Caledonia Games holding an unknown wee lass. Mulligan and wife Violet had a long childless marriage but remained together through good times and bad.

During his police career he had few close friends in the department but sought out those in the force that he felt would do his bidding. He also cultivated the company of men with position, power, and influence in the community. While he lived without the obvious trappings of affluence—big house, big car, big boat—Mulligan, always impeccably dressed, socialized with those whose incomes and lifestyles far exceeded the $10,000 per year he earned as police chief.

On taking office Mulligan warned all ranks that any laxity in discipline would be dealt with immediately and severely. Those assigned responsibilities under the new CIB were put on a two-year rotation so that no officer spent more than two years on vice.

Throughout his seven and a half years as chief, Mulligan carried on a running battle with the police union. As the department history points out: "The union never had much time for the new chief. They didn't like the rotation plan and were very upset at the way Mulligan promoted junior men over what they felt were better-qualified senior men. This was to have serious repercussions later."

Less than six months into his command, Mulligan suddenly lost his mentor, the man who had pushed him up the ladder. With Gerry McGeer as mayor, Mulligan's position was secure, but on August 11, 1947, it was a shaken Mulligan who informed the media that Mayor McGeer had been found dead of a heart attack, lying on a sofa at his home on Belmont Avenue. He was 59. A police chauffeur who was to drive McGeer to city hall found the body. Water Mulligan told the media: "This is a terrible shock to us all."

Mulligan, remembering the glowing stories in the newspapers about his predecessor W.W. Foster, catered to the press as long as he felt it was on his side. He objected, however, to adverse criticism and sometimes fought back. In 1948 he complained bitterly about what he felt was unfair coverage in the media and the overplaying of minor crime. "I would point out [that] when criticism takes the form of unnecessary prominence given to crime reports in the press, particularly when written up with the obvious intention of discrediting the police administration, it has a far reaching damaging affect on the reputation of this city as a whole." Mulligan added that he felt the general public was understanding and appreciative and that it knew the police were putting out an honest effort.

Mulligan understood the value of public relations, as his public appearances in pulpits and on stages bore out. *Province* reporter Ed Moyer knew him as well as anyone. He interviewed the chief for the paper's weekend magazine in 1953 and pointed out that Mulligan had headed the department longer than had any other chief. Moyer wrote about Mulligan's approach to the public: "Today his office opens to them all. He listens attentively to their

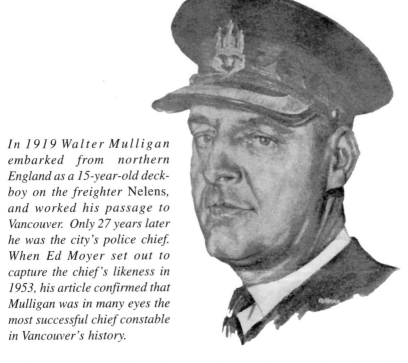

In 1919 Walter Mulligan embarked from northern England as a 15-year-old deck-boy on the freighter Nelens, *and worked his passage to Vancouver. Only 27 years later he was the city's police chief. When Ed Moyer set out to capture the chief's likeness in 1953, his article confirmed that Mulligan was in many eyes the most successful chief constable in Vancouver's history.*

various complaints and fantastic proposals and religious cranks with world-saving formulae follow petty crooks with magnified beefs into his inner sanctum. He is a paradox who mingles at ease with the greatest and shoots the breeze companionably with characters whose idiosyncrasies would try the patience of Job." Moyer added that Mulligan, while under attack from his critics, "neither lost his dignity nor yielded an inch."

Walter Mulligan frequently rode a horse in the Pacific National Exhibition parade, on one occasion asking the Police Commission to buy him new riding boots. The mounted squad was disbanded in 1949 as the car took over, but it was re-established in 1953 to fulfil duties in Stanley Park and at special events.

A growing city meant more work for the police, and the number of calls coming in over the police radio reached 65,000 per year in 1949. Mulligan established a police-training academy, and each new recruit was required to attend it. In-service training was also provided, but it was underfunded and inadequate. The police department's official history states that Mulligan made a number of positive changes. He formed a youth squad to combat increasing juvenile crime, and he introduced a crime prevention program and a traffic-safety plan involving the public. He had a revolver range built in the headquarters' basement. Mulligan accepted many public-speaking engagements and won the respect of audiences across the country. For his efforts he was elected president of the Chief Constables Association of Canada in 1953.

In a handwritten biographical form he completed for the *Province*, Walter Mulligan stated that he was a member of Christ Church Cathedral, a director of the John Howard Society and the district council of Boy Scouts, and a member of the Vancouver East Lions Club and the Board of Trade. He was president of the Vancouver Optimist Club in 1947. Mulligan had played an active part in his community, both in the right places and in the wrong ones.

During Mulligan's tenure, the department grew from slightly over 400, to 600, and then, by 1953, to 683 men and women. This growth was only partly due to the union's insistence in 1948 that the workweek be reduced to 40 hours, a move bitterly opposed by Mulligan.

As the official history states: "By 1953, things were starting to fall apart for Chief Mulligan. Rumours had begun to circulate that he was too friendly with people involved in illegal gambling and there was major discontent within the department." The union, always hostile, maintained an ongoing war against his system of promotions on merit, claiming that favouritism was causing serious morale problems. It disliked him intensely.

The mounting pressure on Mulligan began to show. Reporters noticed that his former open-door policy had changed and that he had become more close-mouthed. More than 40 years later, veteran reporter Charlie King recalled his days at the *Province*, when Mulligan frequently dropped into the press room at city hall after attending meetings with the Police Commission. Mulligan had often regaled newsmen with anecdotes about the police and life in general. By 1954 such visits had all but ceased. One reporter described him during the inquiry proceedings as a prominent figure, from the Vancouver Club to the Smiling Buddha in Chinatown, and "the best police chief money could buy."

Mulligan's methods had failed to produce the desired results: crime in Vancouver continued to increase, violence escalated, and criticism was heaped on his broad shoulders.

4.   Mulligan Battles Crime Wave

Mayor Fred Hume promises to "uproot gangland criminals."

A Vancouver newspaper

A series of disastrous events leading up to the Tupper Inquiry adversely affected the reputation of the chief, the Police Commission, and the force. Vancouver was hit by a spectacular crime wave accompanied by an unprecedented level of violence. Competition and growth in the drug trade triggered much of this. The drug situation also fostered a string of bank holdups carried out by addicts in need of cash. Police cars frequently raced through town on the heels of robbers. Judges handed out tough sentences that included time in jail and the lash; for some it was the death penalty. Still the crime wave continued. Magistrate Oscar Orr talked of a reign of terror as he dealt with two men who burst into a house wielding knives in a 1950s-style "home invasion."

Mulligan's demise was hastened by the spectacular murder of Danny Brent. On September 15, 1954, his bullet-riddled body was found near the tenth green, a 30-yard chip shot short of the hole, on the UBC Golf Course. It was as close as Brent ever got to higher education. At 42, he was head waiter at the Press Club and vice-president of the Club, Cabaret and Construction Camp Culinary and Service Employees Union, Local 240—a small group with a big name. Danny was also an ex-convict and a drug dealer. Police who knew him well said he was a "wholesaler," the go-between for the big suppliers and the peddlers who hustled drugs by the cap on the streets. Brent's murder touched off a new phase in the drug wars. There had been previous killings, but Brent was the first to be taken for a ride in true gangster style. Police said his shooting had the earmarks of a professional job. The killers even stuffed a copy of the morning paper down his pants, presumably to stop the blood from his wounds from spilling onto their car seat.

Brent's criminal record went back 20 years. In 1941 he was sentenced to seven years in prison for an Edmonton safe-cracking. Prior to his death he had worked at the Press Club for five years and was known to patrons as a friendly guy, a host, and a bouncer rolled into one. The Press Club was a misnomer. Located on Beattie near Dunsmuir, it was near the major newspapers but was, in reality, a sleezy commercial joint. A mural in the Press Club set the style of the hang-out, showing a gambler slumped over a card table with a knife in his back and his head next to an uneaten sandwich from which a reporter was stealing a pickle. Journalists seldom visited the Press Club, preferring their own Newsmens' Club or nearby beer parlours in the Commercial, Dominion, or Lotus hotels.

Friends said Brent usually carried lots of cash, as much as $3,000. When police searched his body they reported finding only $1.50, but the victim was still wearing his expensive wristwatch. Mulligan's murder investigators believed Brent had been shot elsewhere, driven to the golf course, and dumped. He was shot in the body and in the head. The *Sun* said exactly 32 men and 15 women attended Brent's funeral, where he lay in an open casket. Even heavy makeup could not fully mask the bullet wound in his cheek. The papers had a field day with the gangster-style killing. Investigators later discovered his strongbox, containing a large amount of heroin, but the killers had vanished. Police theorized that either Brent was slain by a gang trying to move in on his territory or he had reneged on a drug debt. In any case, the fact that the killers were never found reflected badly on the reputation of Mulligan and his men.

The CIB had better luck a few weeks after Brent's fatal ride. "Silent Bill" Semenik was snatched and bundled into a car. He was heading for a one-way ride to Stanley Park but scrambled out of the car when it stopped momentarily for traffic. Bullets fired from the car whistled around the fleeing Semenik, and he was wounded in the leg. But luck was with him and he was saved by a patrolling policeman. The two gunmen fled. Eddie Sherban was arrested while trying to hide neck deep in the waters of the harbour. Don Marcoux, a minor league hockey player, was arrested later, and both were charged with attempted murder.

Semenik was a drug peddler and longtime criminal, described in newspaper accounts as a graduate of some of the toughest jails in the United States. Bald, bespectacled, 51-year-old Semenik didn't look the part of the lifetime crook he was. He had been released from the BC penitentiary only a few months earlier. While Semenik was recovering in hospital from the Stanley Park shooting, police charged him with another trafficking offence. During his trial Semenik mugged for the press and spectators and told jokes, but his good humour left him when he was sentenced to 10 years.

During the trial of Eddie Sherban and Don Marcoux for attempted murder,

Semenik acquired his nickname, "Silent Bill." He refused to testify against them, telling the court that his life in the pen wouldn't be long if he did. It was frustrating for Mulligan, his men, and the prosecutor's office. The police made the arrests, but justice was never served because "Silent Bill" wouldn't sing. Poor Bill got an additional three months for refusing to testify. He watched his alleged killers walk out of court free men.

While Semenik was in court, an event occurred that rocked Vancouver and shook officialdom. A bomb shredded an expensive car on a quiet city street. Jack Leonhard, suspected by police of being part of the drug trade, was thrown 20 feet by the blast—his back was broken and he later had a leg amputated. The car was a twisted wreck. Windows were blown out for blocks around and the roar of the explosion was heard two miles away. Leonhard, 38, claimed he was an ordinary salesman, but police said he sold drugs. Mayor Fred Hume, in office since January 1951, linked the Leonhard murder attempt to the killing of Brent and the attempted murder of Semenik and promised to "uproot gangland criminals."

Things were becoming difficult for Mulligan and his men, who were being severely criticised for not finding the crooks. Under pressure from the Police Commission, Mulligan beefed up the drug squad. He went to Ottawa in March 1955 to testify before a Senate committee probing the drug situation in Canada. In defence of his position as chief of the "drug capital" of the country, Mulligan surprised some by suggesting that the country's 3,000 known criminal addicts—about half of whom were in Vancouver—should be segregated in a self-contained colony, maybe on an island. Mulligan told the committee that in his 27 years of police work he had never come across a successfully reformed addict. Mulligan wanted to lock them all up and throw away the key. However, he also suggested a system to provide free drugs to help users control their habit and to reduce crime in Vancouver. He blamed the drug crisis for about 60 percent of the city's recent crime wave, which was costing various levels of government about $10 million per year. He claimed the city's addict population was increasing by about 10 percent a month, that most of the drugs came from Mexico, and that the average addict used three caps of heroin a day (costing four dollars each).

Mulligan produced figures for the Senate committee that listed drug arrests in 1954 at 1,158—a tremendous increase from the 200 made the year he first became chief. He also accused the media of exaggerating the situation. The *Province* hit back with an editorial quoting from the police department's annual report. It listed 48 robberies (including 19 armed holdups in which two banks lost more than $41,000), 248 stolen cars, and 922 miscellaneous thefts in the preceding year. The editorial concluded: "If anybody is exaggerating it is Mulligan."

The 23-man Senate committee visited Vancouver and took another swing at Mulligan and his department. Chairman Tom Reid said that lack of enforcement was "wholly responsible" for the city's mounting drug problems. The committee disagreed with the chief's suggestion for a system of free drugs for addicts, labelling it a "retrograde" step. It recommended the introduction of provincial drug centres, stiffer penalties for addicts, and life sentences for traffickers convicted of a second offence. Reid's committee also advocated both giving sentences of the "utmost severity" for the importation of drugs and segregating addicts from other prisoners. A sweeping educational program was proposed, involving medical authorities as well as parent-teacher organizations. The report got a lukewarm reception from the provincial government in Victoria, which feared that it would cost too much to implement.

Amid the mounting criticism there was one Mulligan success; the arrest of a young man found guilty of the robbery and murder of a Chinese grocer. The accused won a retrial, and in the spring of 1955, John Diefenbaker came to town. Canada's future prime minister, then a not-too-well-known lawyer and Conservative MP from Saskatchewan, defended the young man. "Dief," as fiery and theatrical in court as he was later in the House of Commons, was partially successful, as the accused was found guilty of a reduced charge of manslaughter and sentenced to 20 years in prison.

City Prosecutor Stewart McMorran was in for a busy summer. In addition to evaluating witnesses for the Tupper royal commission he faced a major drug trial in the month of August. While McMorran was often quoted before the inquiry, this is the only scrapbook morsel in which he is pictured.

Not all killers had the benefit of John Diefenbaker as their lawyer, and Mulligan's department was operating in an era of the hangman, the lash, and long sentences. Depending on their views on capital punishment, the members of the public read with fascination or horror about the fate of Lawrence Vincent, a 29-year-old carnival worker convicted of strangling a 12-year-old girl. He first attempted suicide with poison that had been smuggled to him. Penitentiary doctors used a stomach pump to save his life so that he could then be hanged. His execution was a gruesome event. Vincent refused sedation. He spat at the hangman and staged a three-minute struggle against having his arms bound. When the warden tried to calm him and suggested he say his prayers, Vincent replied: "I have said my prayers. Don't hold me. I have the greatest respect for you warden, but I will go when I have made up my mind." To the priest in attendance he said, "You have been awfully kind to me." He called the hangman a fat pig and snarled at him, "Just whenever you are ready, pig." The *Sun* reported he attacked the hangman with "bitter tongue and lashing feet" before being dropped through the trap door and down the old elevator shaft that served as the gallows at the prison. The scene was particularly excruciating for Warden Hugh Christie, who was personally opposed to the death penalty.

Tough sentencing was not reserved only for murderers. On the court house bench Mr. Justice J.V. Clyne had a cold stare that could frighten some into instant repentance. During the "drug wars" five gangsters from Montreal enticed a small-time dealer who had become a nuisance into an empty lot near False Creek. They played "chop-sticks" on his legs with an iron bar, smashing them both. Frightened off by a passing motorist, they were later arrested for attempted murder. Clyne gave them 20 years each.

Some judges imposed sentences that entailed half the lashes being administered when the accused went to jail and the other half being administered shortly before release, presumably as a reminder of the pain and cost of repeat offences.

Vancouver's spectacular crime wave, with its bizarre incidents and violence along with severe court justice, attracted new attention from the press. Editors assigned additional reporters to keep a closer eye on Mulligan and his minions. One reporter in particular was closing in on certain irregularities in the department.

5.   The Reporters

Ray Munro and Lou Ruby are going steady. Ray is opening a Vancouver office for Ruby's eastern sin sheet. A flash in the pan?

                    Jack Wasserman, March 10, 1955

In the 1950s the members of Vancouver's fourth estate were always ready to battle governments and authority and often went looking for a scrap. It was ironic that they failed to break the story that became the Mulligan Affair. All the papers, but particularly the *Vancouver Province*, had reporters with good contacts in the police department who had heard the rumours and the gossip. Despite the fact that some journalists on the police beat had a liking for Mulligan and knew him well, they were still anxious to write the stories of graft, corruption, and bookmaking that would make headlines and bring them bylines. They tried, but the only stories printed skirted the real issues.

It was the publishers who hesitated and blanched at the prospect of a libel suit. This story was hot, maybe too hot to handle, capable of rocking the political scene from city hall to the legislature in Victoria. Most of the early reports were based on rumour and unnamed sources, and the culprit was the personable and popular police chief, the longest lasting in the department's troubled history. On the surface Walter Mulligan looked good, and he had made sweeping changes in the department. The dailies called in corporate lawyers who fed the publishers' fears about lawsuits if the stories were wrong. If they were sued and lost, the costs could be staggering.

Time and again, rumours and reports of skullduggery from Walter Mulligan on down kept landing on city desks, but the publishers killed them. Editors and reporters continued to go after more facts and corroboration for what loomed as Vancouver's biggest story of the decade.

This story became an obsession for one aggressive, headline-seeking reporter/photographer—*Province* employee Ray Munro. When the managing editor backed off the story, despite Munro's insistence that he had the goods on Mulligan, sparks flew. The young crusader quit and went looking for someone who would print his story.

This was the mid-1950s, when newspapers played a far greater role in the community than they do today. Each one had its own stars, well known, widely read, and not without clout. The competition was enhanced by the sheer number of journalists involved. There were nearly 100 reporters on each of the two afternoon dailies, the *Province* and the *Sun*. Other writers toiled on the *Vancouver Herald* until its demise in 1957 or on the *New Westminster Columbian*, which survived a while longer. There were also a limited number of radio news reporters, while black-and-white TV news was not yet timely, frequently suffering from snowy periods.

Newspaper staffs included those who were already celebrities on the local or national scene as well as those who would soon leave their mark in Canadian history books. A couple of recent university graduates were Jack Wasserman and Pat Carney, while established columnists included Barry Mather, Jean Howarth, Eric Nicol, and Jack Scott. Numbers of newly arrived "Brits" fresh from the pages of such papers as the *Manchester Guardian* or Glasgow's *Evening Times* were well represented by Jack Webster, Paddy Sherman, Jack Brooks, and Doug Collins. Simma Holt was starting her second decade at the *Sun*. These are a few of many who went on to make names for themselves in writing or in politics.

The two big dailies ruled the news roost in a rash, brash, colourful, and controversial way. Each paper had a mid-morning edition, followed by late street-sales versions and a going home final. The *Herald*, the city's sole morning paper, constantly struggled for survival. After its demise it remained a publication remembered fondly by its staff, a number of whom went on to top reporting jobs across the country. Radio news covered mostly local events in brief flashes.

The *Province*, the oldest and largest daily until 1950, was billed as "Vancouver's Family Newspaper." The young marrieds of the city read it, as their parents had before them, in preference to the upstart *Sun*, "Vancouver's Only Home-Owned Newspaper," which was locally owned by the Cromie family and prone to sensationalism. This was encouraged by publisher Don Cromie, who was engaged in a circulation war that never ended. Both papers were lively and often irreverent.

As the last half of the century began, this situation changed. The *Province*, a part of the Southam chain, was hit by a strike. Unions that operated the linotype machines and presses struck Southam's Winnipeg paper and called for support from their Vancouver comrades. Union members across the country were called on to stop buying Southam newspapers, and many did. In Vancouver the unionized workforce switched its allegiance to the *Sun*.

Sun *Publisher Don Cromie (left) liked a splashy front page and found the police corruption inquiry great for business. Almost fifty years after joining the* Sun, *Simma Holt (right) recalled meeting "the two greatest journalists I have ever known—city editor Himie Koshovey and managing editor Hal Straight" during the Mulligan era.*

The *Province* hired strikebreakers to keep the presses rolling, and in the end everyone lost. The strike continued until 1953. By then *Sun* circulation had soared to nearly 200,000, on a par with what it is today, and the *Province* did its best to catch up. After the strike ended, newsroom rivalry increased as the circulation war accelerated.

Many of the nearly 200 writers at the two papers were young and enthusiastic, mentored by old-timers who, between them, had worked on almost every paper in Canada. A young Pat Carney, later to become a short-fused Conservative MP, Cabinet minister, and senator, was assigned to do a story plugging the circus and ended up posing for the camera while riding an elephant.

Jack Wasserman, the *Sun*'s roving gossip columnist, epitomized the era. His name still appears at the corner of Hornby and Georgia in Vancouver on a sign reading "Wasserman's Beat." At times his column read like a collaboration between Damon Runyon and Beatrix Potter, a combination of street-smart talk and the naiveté of the Flopsy and Mopsy creator. With an ample nose, a ready smile, big round glasses, and slicked down hair, laid back Wasserman was a well known figure in Vancouver's clubs and cabarets. While making his rounds Wasserman befriended theatregoers, entertainers, many of Mulligan's men, and the odd bookmaker and bookie. A night person who slept days, he was a chain-smoker, as were most of his newsroom buddies. Wasserman offered them all a dollar an item for his column. They were gladly supplied but hardly for the money: the tid-bits were often designed to promote a friend or draw blood from an enemy. Jack Wasserman wrote about them all as well as about any "purty hat-check chick" that caught his eye.

Even Jack's personal life fuelled many a column. *Sun* readers lived through (survived, many felt) Wasserman's meeting, marriage, and divorce of his first wife, Californian Fran Gregory. They met, appropriately, at the Cave, Vancouver's Hornby Street nightclub, where Fran was booked to sing beneath the papier maché stalactites. Many thought Fran was mediocre at best, but to Wasserman she was Mitzi Gaynor and

Girl reporter joins the circus---for a day!

One slow Wednesday during the inquiry, young Province *reporter Pat Carney "donned a frilly costume," joined the Clyde Beatty circus for a day, and rode atop "Babe," a 70-year-old elephant.*

Doris Day rolled into one. In April 1954, his column read: "[The] Cave is featuring a relatively unknown singer named Fran Gregory and Isy Walters figures he has a potential star in his place. He could be right." The next day Wasserman wrote: "Went back for second look at the Cave's Fran Gregory and still don't believe it. Wow." For several years, Jack, Fran, and *Sun* subscribers got to know each other well.

In February of 1955 the *Sun* hailed the 28-year-old Wasserman as its top police and crime reporter, and a drug series appeared stressing a terrible toll in human misery. "City Exposed as Stronghold of World Narcotic Ring" read the headline after Wasserman interviewed drug experts in New York. Vancouver's police chief was not mentioned.

The publishers still had Walter Mulligan on hold, but at the *Province* Ray Munro was working up an irrational hatred of the chief and some members of his beleaguered department. Egotistical; without fear of God, death, or the city editor; and prone to exaggeration if it suited his purpose, Munro was not the most respected newsman among his peers. But he made headlines and that sold newspapers. With all the first-class reporters working in Vancouver, it was ironic that it was Ray Munro who would be Walter Mulligan's nemesis.

Munro was born in Montreal in 1922. When he published his own autobiography in 1985 he added the middle initial "Z," which was not in evidence at his birth. Like Zorro as he galloped across the countryside performing good deeds, Munro saw nothing wrong with going to any excess to stamp his mark on the world. In his view the truth was there to be stretched; fame was there to be sought; and people were there to be impressed, intimidated, or blackmailed—whichever was necessary at the time.

In his book, *The Sky's No Limit*, the jacket blurb boldly states: "Ray Munro is one of the most honoured Canadians in history. Among his more than 400 honours he claims 100 honourary citizenships, 19 life-saving presentations, the Order of Canada, the Order of St. John of Jerusalem, The Order of Polaris, 61 FAI aviation records and numerous other orders, decorations and medals." There's no doubt Munro was resourceful, imaginative, brave, a skilled photographer, and a capable pilot, but it would be no mean feat to achieve all he claimed. Extreme exaggeration and galloping excess were his trademarks.

Typical of Munro was a newspaper story he wrote under the headline, "I flew with Badder in the Battle of Britain." The Battle of Britain was fought in the skies over southern England in the summer and fall of 1940, when Winston Churchill immortalized Spitfire and Hurricane pilots who battled the German Luftwaffe as "the few" to whom so many owed so much. Munro was a pilot, but he didn't get to Britain until 1941. He would have loved to have been one of "the few," but he was not. Why he was discharged from the RCAF in 1942 is not clear, although he admitted to being in three crashes. During the Tupper Inquiry, a defence lawyer suggested he was discharged for psychological reasons, a comment that brought an angry tirade from the mighty Munro.

After his air force discharge he went to work as a photographer for the *Toronto Star*, where he displayed considerable talent. Volatile and incapable of staying long in one job, Munro moved west in 1947 and took a job with the *Sun*. His propensity for change led him, within a year, to a partnership with well-known Vancouverite Art Jones in a firm known as Artray Photography. The partnership soon ended, and Munro moved to the *Province* in 1949, where he won a National Newspaper Award for photography.

Ray Munro always sought the limelight and, in his own mind, was an expert at whatever he tried—a trait that often irked his colleagues. On the *Province* he was both reporter and photographer. Fellow newsmen remember Munro in different ways. He had a peculiar sense of humour and thought it

Great friends for thirty years, "the two Jacks," Wasserman (left) and Webster worked together at the Sun *until Webster handed Hal Straight his notice in 1953.*

Himie Koshovey "with Ray Munro who had a couple of Russian hats left over from some party." Munro, intent on being legendary, was occasionally accused of writing his own legends.

hilarious to sneak up on a colleague and cut off his tie with a pair of scissors. Even now reporter Charlie King gets miffed when he thinks of an expensive gift from his wife that Munro destroyed. "There was much to like him for and much to dislike in him. My balance was in the dislike," recalled King. Another ex-*Province* colleague, Gordon Purver, remembers meeting Munro in Montreal. A far-fetched scheme to mine gold from the St. Lawrence River was Munro's fixation at that time, Purver said.

Himie Koshevoy, long-time *Sun, Province,* and *Herald* newsroom boss, much admired by the many who worked for him and appreciated his puckish sense of humour, had this to say when asked to contribute to Munro's obituary: "He was known as a very handsome man, good looking and very persuasive with the fair sex. He was very friendly towards me. But then he wrote a book and said I was a mean little bastard. I was never mean towards him. I was always suspicious of him."

Munro was the type who couldn't write a story about the Salvation Army without supposedly receiving death threats or being slugged with a tambourine by a mystery woman dressed in dark blue. He went out of his way to be pictured with celebrities and, on one occasion, managed to get himself in a photo with Marilyn Monroe. He had his car fitted with lights and special equipment and said it was an emergency ambulance.

Ray was fascinated with guns and got a permit to transport a handgun to practice sessions. He preferred to leave the impression it was fully licensed and necessary for his own protection, but a bulge in his jacket often concealed only an empty holster.

Munro liked action. He often mixed with the lowlife in Vancouver's bootleg dives and betting hangouts. He also liked policemen. It was from ordinary cops and other reporters that Munro learned many had a loathing for Chief Mulligan, and he soon adopted and magnified their views.

As a newsman Ray's mind moved in mysterious ways, and he had a style and approach that would have made him a perfect employee for today's English tabloids or the *National Enquirer.* In August 1949, Munro's escapades produced the spectacular "Stanley Park Caper," the kind of story that young, and not so young, reporters dream about. Munro learned from a contact at the police station that a series of rapes in Stanley Park had a similar "modus operandi." Mulligan's men had failed to catch the rapist, and Munro decided he would solve the crimes himself.

He went to *Province* managing editor Bill Forst with his idea, and, as a result, Munro and another staff writer, Don McLean (who was disguised as a woman), sat in a car in Stanley Park one August night. Munro was carrying his .45 automatic. At 2:00 a.m. they heard an approaching car, and flashlights were shone into their faces. As Munro told it, he and McLean burst out of the

In his autobiography Ray Munro claimed to have piloted a sight-seeing flight for Rory Calhoun (in background) and Marilyn Monroe and to have later joined them for dinner.

At his retirement party Himie Koshevoy was flanked by Hal Straight, Jack Wasserman, Jack Webster, and Paddy Sherman. Ray Munro was twenty years gone from the Vancouver scene.

car taking four men by surprise, who at once fled the scene. Munro fired a shot but hit only a nearby tree. A piece of bark flew off and hit one of the intruders in the leg. He went down and was grabbed by the two newsmen. Munro took a picture, they put the attacker in the trunk of their car, and then they called police. The would-be rapist was John Kenneth Clark, a 32-year-old labourer from Port Coquitlam. Police found his truck nearby and a notebook listing the licence numbers of the cars in which his victims had been parked. Clark was sentenced to 15 years and 10 lashes but refused to name his three accomplices. Police knew who they were but had no evidence against them. Walter Mulligan was mortified, while Munro bathed in accolades and attention. It was not the only time the chief would be a victim of the unrelenting reporter.

The Stanley Park caper was a great newspaper story, Munro at his best, and he didn't hesitate to pat himself heartily on the back. The caper got big play in the *Province*, and it ran in most North American newspapers as well as in popular detective magazines.

Another Munro story, this one occurring in 1954, helped to cook Mulligan's goose. There had been a killing in Vancouver's drug wars, and Munro was sitting in a Main Street beverage room that he described as "a scab among a festering collection of decrepit buildings, cheap cafes, three-dollar whores and the bulk of Canada's drug-addict population." While pondering ways to "flush out the killers," he bought a lottery ticket from a waiter. At the time lotteries were illegal in British Columbia and Munro began to wonder if his ticket was real or phoney. He'd never heard of the Western Canadian Employees Sweep. Bill Forst assigned several reporters to check out the alleged names of winners on a Sweep prize sheet. They couldn't find any. This led to a banner headline and the story that a phoney million-dollar lottery was raking in the dough. The *Sun*, unable to disprove the *Province* story, came up with its own scandals, and for weeks readers were swamped with tales of phoney lotteries.

When the *Province* criticised Mulligan, the *Sun* cozied up to him and ran features maintaining that the public had not been informed about the racket because the department was hot on the trail of the perpetrators. In one instance the chief claimed he had told the Police Commission that one of the top ticket-sellers was the wife of a senior city fireman.

Ray Munro reported getting his usual number of death threats. Alderman Bill Orr, unrelated to Police Commissioner Oscar Orr, claimed that the police had known about the phoney lottery racket for years but had done nothing, although he backed away from any charges that the police had deliberately "repressed" information. The spotlight, however, was now aimed firmly at the department, and Walter Mulligan was asked for a full report. The Police Commission failed to make public the contents of the report but issued a brief statement saying that it found "no evidence of suppression on the part of any of those officers who had occasion from time to time to deal with this matter." They agreed with Mulligan's admission that there had been "laxity," which he promised to clean up. A few houses were raided, phoney tickets found, some people charged and fined. There was also panic in the illegal lottery business. In Grand Forks, a town in the Kootenays, a batch of Irish Hospital Sweepstake tickets were found scattered along the railway tracks, dumped by a frightened dealer. A *Province* editorial called for "no more obvious laxity" from the chief, and the writer was astonished at the way the commission was allowing Mulligan to shrug off the matter.

The lottery caper quietly faded away. Editorial writers and local politicians agreed that it was Ottawa's fault. What was needed was a sensible lottery law within the federal criminal code.

Munro's brush with fame, coupled with his dislike of Mulligan, spurred him on. Out to dig up everything he could find, Munro discussed his concerns with former fellow air force flyer Eddie Moyer, a versatile *Province* reporter and artist. Moyer had been on the police beat for a number of years and shared his contacts with Munro. In addition the ever-eager Munro did his own sleuthing with underworld characters as well as cops in the department. By early 1955, Munro was churning out his own version of police department irregularities. Despite Munro's previous spectacular successes, managing editor Forst had reservations about the new series of articles. He worried that Munro's obsessive nature was clouding his thinking and, after discussions with company lawyers, publisher Arthur Moscarella, and assistant publisher Ross Munro (no relation), Forst turned down Ray's new inflammatory series of articles. In long, soul-searching discussions with Bill Forst, Munro fought for his stories, but finally, annoyed that they might never see the light of day, he quit and took them with him. He knew there was little chance of a warm reception at the *Sun,* where his sudden departure earlier had irked editors. Its reporters had turned in similar information to editors, but once again the threat of libel loomed large. Then Munro found a publisher.

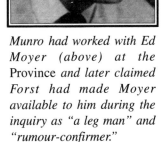

Munro had worked with Ed Moyer (above) at the Province *and later claimed Forst had made Moyer available to him during the inquiry as "a leg man" and "rumour-confirmer."*

From his days on the *Toronto Star*, Munro knew where there was a likely market for the stories he wanted to peddle. Toronto in the postwar period had several racy tabloids that thrived on scandal,

Province managing editor Bill Forst, a leading figure in Vancouver journalism, had a difficult task trying to manage Ray Munro. Nevertheless the reporter later described Forst as having "the ability to get the very best from every member of his staff."

Betty (Hortin) O'Keefe was hired by Bill Forst in 1950 and wrote for the magazine section throughout the Tupper Inquiry.

blood, and gore. They operated on the edge of libel, owning few seizable assets should they lose a suit and be charged with damages.

Prominent among the tabs was *Flash*, whose publisher, Lou Ruby, had a personal life as colourful as the stories his publications ran. *Flash* had been operating for close to 20 years, with offices on the third floor of an ancient building on Adelaide Street. Ruby bought the rag for $500 in 1947 and boasted that, despite more than its share of troubles, *Flash* had never paid out a nickel in damages. He claimed he had been offered $500,000 for his publishing concern.

While knowing a good deal about Toronto lowlife, Ruby also liked to mingle with the city's upper crust and horsey set, who found him as flashy as his paper. A grey-haired hustler, he liked to show off his wealth. He drove a sky-blue Cadillac and bought the Stephen Leacock estate at Brewery Bay near Orillia in wealthy cottage country north of Toronto. Local residents were suspicious of Ruby and his possible plans for subdivision, but he astutely won them over by selling the house and Leacock's papers for a very reasonable amount to the local historical society.

Munro and Ruby were two of a kind, the *Flash* publisher being as flamboyant as the reporter, but with a lot more money in the bank. Ruby had his own stable of eight horses and lost money publishing a magazine called *The Thoroughbred*. According to a description in the *Toronto Star*, his love of creatures equine followed through to the yellow curtains with a purple horse design and gaudy fittings in his Adelaide Street office. Ruby's fascination with the word *flash* included Flash Gordon, an aged bay gelding that won a $1,000 jumper's sweepstake at the Canadian National Exhibition Horse Show in the late 1950s. Ruby lived in the expensive Forest Hills district of Toronto and died in 1979. His son Clayton is today one of Ontario's leading criminal lawyers.

Ruby came to Vancouver to finalize an agreement with Munro. Jack Wasserman, in his March 10 *Sun* column, wrote: "Ray Munro and Lou Ruby are going steady. Ray is opening a Vancouver office for Ruby's eastern sin sheet. A flash in the pan?"

As Munro discussed a working agreement with Ruby, Walter Mulligan was under increasing pressure and took steps to protect himself. In a confidential letter on April 5 he told the police commissioners that he had been tipped that two officers, three Vancouver newsmen, and a Social Credit MLA were out to discredit him and the force. He said they would allege payoffs for gambling and "other vices." No names were ever made public when the letter was discussed during the inquiry—an event that was now only a matter of weeks away.

Three years earlier, in 1952, Walter Mulligan had sent the commissioners another letter alleging that some of his officers were conspiring against him. The commissioners had paid little attention to that complaint, suggesting that Mulligan's officers were Mulligan's problem.

The first Vancouver weekly edition of *Flash* hit the streets on June 15. It was one of several editions published during the early weeks of summer. At times short on facts and long on innuendo, speculation, and superlatives, it contained stories with enough punch to produce immediate reader reaction. The scene was set when one of the first headlines shouted: "The Lid is Off Vancouver Vice and Its Allies." The tabloid went on to proclaim: "Starting this week, Ray Munro, veteran reporter and head of *Flash*'s West Coast Bureau, will bring you the true story of how police corruption, City Hall, conniving and Gangland money turned Vancouver into Canada's Crime Centre, the story it took months of patient checking to uncover, the story which Munro hammered out on his typewriter as paid bodyguards shielded his every move, the blazing story of the rape of a city!"

It was purple prose and searing sensationalism, and *Flash* promised a lot more:

- Read about the Police Chief and the Vanishing Piggy Bank
- Read of the Society Playboy's Sinister Double Life
- Read Why Vancouver Today is Hop Head Heaven
- Read of the Scarlet Women and Their Highly Placed Lovers
- Read of the Senior Detective Who Spilled His Guts to Victoria
- Read How the Politicians Sold Out You the Public

- Read How the Syndicate Captured City Hall
- Read the Price Tags on Vancouver Officialdom
- Read Why Press Photographers are Banned at Police Courts

The tabloid concluded: "Read the Whole Shocking Story in *Flash*."

The allegations rocked the city, and local media knew they'd been had. Sergeant Len Cuthbert, already a worried man, read the edition and succumbed to despair.

Within hours the Police Commission held an emergency meeting. The *Sun* reported that the commissioners looked "glum" going into the meeting, although Mayor Fred Hume commented: "I have 100-per-cent confidence in Chief Mulligan and his department." His confidence didn't last. The mayor said he would be interested in knowing more about *Flash*'s contention that a syndicate had taken over city hall. Commissioner Rey Sargent noted that "it [was] one thing after another." Magistrate Oscar Orr said that he was tired of attending a meeting every time a paper said something was wrong with the department, but he agreed that "these [were] serious charges."

Mulligan attended the hastily called meeting and was advised he should get a lawyer. The chief told reporters he had hired Senator J.W.deB. Farris, QC, a respected partner in one of the city's leading law firms. Maintaining there was a deliberate attempt to discredit himself and the force, Mulligan hit back: "I have a pretty good idea how this whole matter came to this publication and where the attack comes from and I am going after the source." He added he had nothing to hide and was not "afraid to face anything that anybody brought out."

The commission issued a brief statement asking anyone with information about wrongdoing to contact the city prosecutor. For the first time the police commissioners publicly mentioned the "secret" investigation of the department five years earlier, stating that an inquiry into alleged illegal activities had produced nothing: "That is where the matter stands today." Mayor Hume declined to answer questions about his confidence in Walter Mulligan.

The Vancouver media were scrambling. Wasserman ran an item that a man had been "worked over" after the *Flash* story appeared. His opposition, columnist Dan Ekman, reported in the *Province* that the beating was merely the result of a row between unions. Wasserman also wrote that, following the exposé, a veteran member of the detective squad was on the verge of a nervous breakdown. It wasn't long before Cuthbert's actions confirmed this story.

On June 23 Mulligan sued *Flash* and Munro. Farris said there had been the "grossest kind of libel," although he stated that if Mulligan were a private citizen he would have suggested forgetting the stories. It was only after the Mulligan suit that the *Sun* plucked up its courage and reprinted a page of

Flash as it had appeared on the streets. It would be nine months before the courts dismissed Mulligan's suits, assessing the costs to him.

The next day, June 24, Vancouver was stunned by Detective Sergeant Len Cuthbert's attempted suicide, which added credibility to the *Flash* allegations. All three Vancouver dailies finally jumped on the story, and the radio stations broke in with news as it developed. There were pictures of the wounded cop being taken from the Main Street police station on a gurney. *Sun* reporter Ron Thornber was working the police beat and knew the detective personally. He wrote that only the day before Cuthbert had said to him: "I am going to blow my brains out or something. That is the only way to settle the problems I've got."

Within hours of the shooting, the Police Commission called another emergency meeting behind closed doors. Attorney General Robert Bonner was called in during the nine hours of discussion and asked to authorize a public inquiry into the entire affair. The next day, when Mulligan was told of the decision, he stoically asked to be placed on paid leave. Superintendent Alan Rossiter was named acting chief.

A public announcement said the inquiry, under Section 3 of the Public Inquiries Act, would be held as soon as possible in the court house. It was ordered because "allegations suggestive of corruption in the police department of the city of Vancouver and of laxity in the enforcement of the criminal code of Canada by that department have recently been made and are of such a nature as to disturb the confidence of the public in the police department of the city of Vancouver and its administration."

The Police Commission asked that the truth or falsity of the accusations be probed. Reginald H. Tupper, QC, now a partner in a prominent Vancouver law firm, was named the sole inquiry commissioner. J.G.A. Hutcheson, QC, age 59, was later appointed chief commission counsel. The retired dean had the "widest terms of reference" and the power to hold private sessions (if necessary) in what soon became known as the Tupper Commission inquiry into police corruption or, simply, the Tupper Inquiry.

Ray Munro, the renegade reporter who wouldn't go away, was all smiles and walking tall. Behind him were a pack of publishers, frantic managing editors, and scurrying reporters—all trying to catch up.

Vancouver's classic court house was opened in 1911 and redefined the growth of the city centre. Its front entrance (middle) was adorned by two lions, long symbols of British justice. The panorama below shows the original building and the newer West Wing (to the left). In 1979 these buildings became home to the Vancouver Art Gallery. As a relic of days past the Assize Courtroom, where Tupper (right) chaired his inquiry, remains intact.

6.   The Probe Begins

It made my mark in Vancouver.

Jack Webster

Capital punishment is no longer imposed amid chilly awfulness in the high-vaulted rooms of Vancouver's old court house, but in 1955 sentences of life or death often echoed through those solemn brooding rooms. While no spectre of the gallows cast shadows on participants during the Tupper Inquiry, for more than seven months (starting in July), this classic building was the centre of a great human drama. The testimony of police, politicians, and lawyers laid bare the inner workings of a racket that had infested much of the city.

Today, the old grey stone building looks so typical of its origins that film makers use it regularly for court-house scenes. Now fronted by lawns and a black stone fountain, it fills a city block in downtown Vancouver on Georgia between Howe and Hornby. It has been converted into the Vancouver Art Gallery, but in 1955 the sedate structure was the legal centre of the province.

Although he was well known and admired in legal circles, Commissioner Tupper's reputation had been earned outside the courtroom as dean of UBC's

Faculty of Law. He was an academic—tall, urbane, and quiet by nature. He came from a pre-eminent Canadian family, being the grandson of Sir Charles Tupper, Prime Minister of Canada and Father of Confederation. His father was also a politician and had been an MP in Sir Charles's Cabinet. Reginald Tupper had reason to be proud of his Canadian heritage. When his grandfather's government was defeated in the 1890s, the young Tupper moved with his family to Vancouver. Raised on the West Coast, he was enrolled in his

From the
McMorran
Scrapbook

late teens as a cadet in the Royal Navy College in England, where he remained until he was discharged on medical grounds.

He was able to join the Canadian army as a machine gunner in the First World War, however, and was badly wounded in the battle of Ypres. Reg Tupper had been a defeated Conservative candidate for the riding of North Vancouver in the 1940 federal general election, and the new Social Credit government's selection of him as inquiry commissioner surprised many. It was generally thought that a lawyer with an established reputation cemented through courtroom appearances and highly publicized trials would have been a more appropriate appointee. Tupper's chief counsel, Hutcheson, was also a surprise, a labour lawyer who was not at that time readily recognized by the public.

The Tupper Inquiry opened officially on July 5, less than two weeks after the Cuthbert suicide attempt. Tupper stated that all police with information had a duty to testify, along with anyone else who could assist. He assured them that they had nothing to fear and that those who did not step forward or volunteer to correct any evidence that they knew to be incorrect would be considered delinquent. The police union identified 40 volunteers who offered to testify.

Tupper outlined his responsibilities, stressing that it was his duty to inquire and report. From the outset he made it clear that this was not a court and that he was not going to be bound by trial procedures. He also noted that it would not be a wide-open or "roving" hearing, "but [that] at the same time it [would] not [be] narrowed to just a few allegations." Some statistical information was given about the police department, and then the hearing was adjourned to July 13. It was unlucky 13 for Mulligan, whose world started to fall apart on that day.

That same July 13 marked a new beginning for an apprentice radioman. Former *Sun* reporter Jack Webster would reach thousands of listeners nightly during the Mulligan Affair. They tuned in to CJOR to hear him read what could be up to a five-hour account of inquiry proceedings. "It made my mark in Vancouver," he said many years later when he recalled the hectic days and nights that brought him into the world of radio and, later, BCTV News broadcasting at "5:00 p.m. precisely" each evening.

By the time the inquiry opened the public was entranced, intrigued by newspaper reports and anxious to learn what each day's testimony would reveal. How rotten was the Vancouver police force? How deep were the

---

Day after day, the headlines blared as Vancouver's three dailies jumped on the story. Attorney General Robert Bonner met with Vancouver's police commissioners and decided that the best way to deal with all the events was through a royal commission.

cops into the pockets of local bookies and gamblers? What was to come as the money-loaded drug industry continued its deadly battle for business? Had there been coverups? Were politicians involved, and who were they? As the evidence unfolded, everyone had reason to suspect the tentacles of corruption reached a long, long way. Massive newspaper coverage and Webster's daily reading of his verbatim shorthand notes kept Vancouver and much of the country well informed.

Some of the city's leading lawyers, along with those who would rise to prominence in later years, were hired by the commission; by the flamboyant Ray Munro, who started it all; by Police Chief Mulligan; by police officers; and by a host of other key witnesses. Some of these men were involved in bizarre events far beyond the normal role expected of counsel. For a variety of reasons, at least three lawyers walked out during the inquiry. Neil Fleishman was fed up with his client, Ray Munro; Tom Norris was threatened with blackmail; and Jay Gould left arm in arm with the former chief of police. One young lawyer recently arrived from Britain stepped abruptly into the limelight when he was hired by the police union to defend Len Cuthbert. He was H.A.D. Oliver, who would become one of Vancouver's most respected criminal lawyers, a Justice of the Supreme Court, and, in 1997, BC's new conflict-of-interest commissioner. The Tupper Inquiry was an incredible spectacle.

At the outset, Tupper stated that he had asked the publisher and key staff of the tabloid *Flash* to appear as witnesses, pointing out that, as Ontario residents, they could not be summoned to appear. They declined. Their distributor, Vancouver Magazine Service, decided not to distribute 20,000 copies of one edition of the scandal sheet published during the probe because it felt it might be libelous. The distributor, represented by lawyer G.L. Murray, said it would accept the financial loss.

There were bristling battles on points of law and procedure. Jay Gould, who would represent Mulligan after the departure of Tom Norris (see Chapter 10), challenged Tupper time after time about his handling of the inquiry. Gould protested bitterly about "the torrent of hearsay evidence" that wouldn't be admissible in a regular trial. Tupper always answered that he was conducting the inquiry on the lines of natural justice. He said that his job was to ferret out information, not to establish guilt and lay blame. However, much of the evidence clearly spoke for itself.

An amazed public heard of sweeping concerns about leaks and breaches of confidentiality at the police station as early as 1951 and 1952. One investigating officer, Detective Sergeant Archie Plummer, said he regularly took his papers home at night so they would remain confidential and secure.

Webster's nightly reports grew more intriguing. If the police department resembled the Keystone Kops, the Police Commission was even more slapstick. With the mayor as its chairman, the commission included a magistrate and a judge appointed by the province under the terms of the city charter. Evidence disclosed that this trio had received information from Len Cuthbert as early as 1949 in a bare-your-soul confession that implicated both him and the chief. They ordered a "secret" investigation by a former RCMP officer, T.G. Parsloe. He found the chief and his department cleaner than the driven snow, although the members of the commission had misgivings about the depth and accuracy of his report. Nonetheless they simply accepted it and tucked it quietly away. Until 1955, when their hand was forced by the tabloid *Flash*, these respected civic leaders dithered, swithered, and did nothing despite growing suspicions.

Their conduct is difficult to understand. They were all men of good reputation, but their inept management of the situation led to rumour and speculation. They were not helped much by then attorney general Wismer who had recommended the ex-Mountie who conducted the inadequate investigation. Nor was the commission helped during the Tupper Inquiry, when Wismer suffered chronic memory loss about this secret report, despite the fact he had been consulted about what was obviously a serious matter. Perhaps the commission didn't want another inquiry only two years after the 1947 probe that brought Mulligan to the top spot. Perhaps they knew the people involved too well to be objective. But what could have been worse than leaving the forces of law and order in the hands of a man who each day breached laws he was supposed to enforce? Maybe they hoped it would all sort itself out. It didn't. It couldn't.

Many witnesses who were called before Tupper were victims of the great epidemic of memory loss. Members of the gambling squad suffered from it as they paraded through the inquiry denying everything, admitting nothing. This in spite of the fact that it was evident that the graft operation was not a well kept secret and that rumours abounded at the station and on the streets. Even Ray Munro, the man who wanted everything exposed, succumbed to the disease when confronted by a thundering Tom Norris and threatened with the consequences of his own actions.

Despite this "amnesia," a growing audience was fascinated. Reading and listening to Webster's broadcasts about the Mulligan Affair was enough for some, but for those truly caught up in the unfolding drama, only a seat in the jam-packed courtroom would sate their curiosity. These avid followers made an early trip downtown to mingle daily with the gathering crowd in the old court house.

At the entrance to the Assize Court-room crowds gathered daily to attend the Tupper Inquiry. Court officers were forced to limit entry and turn away many of the curious.

Witness Bob Leatherdale (centre), the first witness to testify, is seen waiting with police union president Sergeant Fred Doughterty (left) and union secretary Dan Brown. With his candour, Leatherdale gave the accusations against Mulligan instant credibility.

7. Crowds Gather—July 13

*Some of the best in the force — including myself — believe
the chief and one or two others are allied with the criminal
element.*

Detective Sergeant Archie Plummer

News of Cuthbert's suicide attempt and the *Flash* stories swept through
Vancouver followed by waves of rumour and speculation. Copies of the
scandal sheet were treasured by those able to buy them before the newsstands
emptied. The *Vancouver Sun* and the *Vancouver Province* still worried about
lawsuits, consulted their lawyers, and refused to repeat the allegations found
in *Flash*. They stuck to the details of Cuthbert's suicide bid, lawyers'
comments, and lists of potential witnesses. Public anticipation soared as
July 13 neared: it was the day slated for the appearance of the first major
witness. Crowds waited for hours outside the court house, and when the
doors opened they stampeded inside. First in got the seats, the rest stood
jam-packed at the rear of the courtroom. It was stifling hot, the middle of a
rare Vancouver heat wave. The fire marshal decided regulations were being
broken and forced protesting people back outside, where they joined hundreds
who hadn't made it through the doors. There was yelling, pushing, and
shoving—even the odd fist fight.

It was at exactly 10:43 a.m. on July 13 when it became crystal clear that
Walter Mulligan had made a bad choice when he picked Detective Sergeant
Bob Leatherdale to include in his expanded graft operation. There were
gasps from the public bench as he testified. Refusing to be roped into
Mulligan's schemes, Leatherdale told the inquiry that there had been a member
of his family on the force for 50 years and that he prized his integrity as a
policeman. In his first day of testimony Leatherdale gave alleged rumours
and innuendo all the credibility the local dailies required. Finally committed
to the story of the year, both evening papers rushed into the street with bold
headlines. The *Sun* cried, "Probe Told Mulligan Sought Deal to Protect

Bootleggers." The *Province* contended, "Mulligan Accused of Part in Bookmaking Bribery Plot." The public was amazed to learn what the Police Commission had known for six years!

Leatherdale was a steady if unspectacular policeman. He was a family man, respected by colleagues for his performance, his support, and his regard for his men. He gave evidence firmly and impressively, without contradiction and without wavering in the heat of cross-examination.

A press table jam-packed with 22 reporters and the crowded galleries hung on every word. Newsmen dashed in relays to phones to dictate their stories. Tupper had refused to allow taping of the evidence, and Webster began filling the first of 60 notebooks he would use during the 40 days of testimony given between July 5 and January 27, 1956, when the Tupper Inquiry finally adjourned.

Mulligan, looking paler and thinner than he had in early June and taking copious notes, sat stoically with his lawyer Tom Norris at the long table in front of the commissioner. Norris was retained to defend Mulligan at the Tupper Inquiry, while J.W.deB. Farris represented him in the suit against Munro and *Flash*. As usual, Mulligan was impeccably dressed. His antagonist Munro was at the other end of the table but left the room shortly after the proceedings began.

The contrasting reactions of Walter Mulligan and Ray Munro were noticeable throughout the inquiry. While Munro wandered in and out, Mulligan never left the table, showing no emotion as charges were levelled against him. The public loved it, and seats in the gallery were soon at such a premium that spectators refused to leave during the lunch hour for fear of losing them.

On the stand Leatherdale said he was promoted to sergeant in 1949 and, shortly afterward, was approached by Mulligan and asked if he was interested in heading the liquor squad. The chief also asked him if he would mind letting a couple of bootlegging establishments stay in business because "it would be good for both of us." Mulligan explained that Cuthbert, who was head of the gambling squad, knew all the details and that, within hours, he visited Leatherdale at his home. In a calm, cool voice Leatherdale related how Cuthbert told him that, as head of the liquor squad, it would be his job "to put pressure on bootleggers not paying for protection." Cuthbert stressed that this would help drive business to those bootleggers who were paying up.

Leatherdale said Cuthbert asked him about bootleggers. "I told him he knew them as well as I did." Cuthbert then named Al Nugent, Peto Nino, Blondie Wallace, Jack Craig, a Mrs. Emily, Hans Burquist, and Joe Celona, saying that would do for a start. Leatherdale continued: "It would have been my job to collect monthly and to split with the chief and the men of the liquor detail." He added: "Cuthbert said we might as well plain talk. The chief

Few photos taken inside the courtroom survived. The courtroom as seen from Tupper's vantage point (top) and (middle) a view of the crowded reporters, table in the background behind Mulligan and his lawyer show the tight quarters in which the drama unfolded. R.H. Tupper, QC, enters his domain as all rise (bottom) and the second day of the inquiry begins.

wants money. He has been in charge for two years and thinks things should open up a little." Cuthbert said he was doing O.K. and so was the chief, both of them doubling their salaries. Mulligan's salary was about $10,000 a year and Cuthbert's was about $5,000. (In later testimony Cuthbert gave a much lower figure for what he received.)

Leatherdale said Cuthbert maintained vice boss Celona was paying $200 a month and that this would soon rise to $300. Leatherdale, who made notes of this conversation, said he went almost immediately to city prosecutor Gordon Scott and told him about the plot. Leatherdale went to see Mulligan two days later and was asked if he had talked to anyone, presumably meaning Cuthbert. Leatherdale said to the chief: "I've had a clean record for a long time and I'm going to keep it so." He turned down the job as head of the liquor squad.

Prosecutor Scott then asked Leatherdale to attend a meeting with two of the police commissioners, Mayor Charles Thompson, and Magistrate Oscar Orr. Again Leatherdale told his story, and Scott suggested that Mulligan had probably just been testing him. A month later, Scott told Leatherdale the commission had spent time and money looking into the allegations but had found "no direct evidence" to confirm Mulligan was taking bribes. In cross-examination Leatherdale stuck to his story: "My personal opinion of the chief was that until 1949 I thought him absolutely on the up and up. I changed my mind." Leatherdale said he believed that at least half the gambling squad of 12 men would have to be on the take if big money was being raked in.

Detective Sergeant Archie Plummer was called to the stand. He turned up the heat on Mulligan and electrified the hearing when he stated firmly: "Some of the best in the force—including myself—believe the chief and one or two others are allied with the criminal element."

Because of staff shortage in the CIB, investigations of serious crimes (such as burglaries and armed robberies) were not being properly followed up.

Tupper asked: "Is the criminal code properly enforced?"

Plummer hesitated then and replied: "Unquestionably it would be better enforced if morale were higher."

Chief Counsel Hutcheson: "Morale is not high?"

Plummer: "I think it is very low. Some of the people on the force, including myself, believe the chief and one or two others are allied with the criminal element. Ninety-five percent of the force know probably little or nothing of that. I think we'll find their gripe is simply a lack of justice. My own morale would be higher if I had a respect for my superiors."

The spectators burst into applause, and Tupper threatened to empty the room if this behaviour was repeated. Mulligan's lawyer, Tom Norris, angrily asked if an organized anti-Mulligan clique was at work.

Plummer then explained that when he took over the gambling squad in 1951, Leatherdale brought him the handwritten notes he had made following his 1949 discussions with Cuthbert. Plummer had the notes typed, took them to Cuthbert's house, and asked if they were accurate. The answer was "Yes." Cuthbert told Plummer that the old man said he had everything "fixed" in Victoria and was close to Wismer. Cuthbert's own view was that Mulligan would be dropped in case of trouble.

Plummer said Cuthbert was emotional and had said: "When Bob turned it down, I said, 'you have guts. I wish I had done the same thing.'" Cuthbert then warned Plummer to "watch out for the guy in the corner. The old man should be well fixed. He is getting paid whether things are fixed or not. It's a kind of insurance."

Plummer continued: "Cuthbert told me I divide with the chief 50/50 but my 50 has to take care of the squad. When Deputy Chief Gordon Ambrose and Criminal Investigation Branch Superintendent Jack Horton saw the chief and he had let them in, I had to pay them $100 a month out of my 50 percent."

Horton's lawyer, Lyle Jestley, interjected: "This is hearsay, twice removed."

Tupper contended: "I think it would be disastrous if hearsay did not come before the commissioner either to lead to evidence or be disposed of."

Bob Leatherdale (top) and Archie Plummer (middle) were quickly painted as the good guys, while clouds of suspicion hung over Assistant Chief Gordon Ambrose (bottom). Cuthbert, with apparently little to gain by the revelation, identified Deputy Chief Gordon Ambrose as being involved in a payoff and being a friend of Joe Celona, described by the Sun *as a "notorious bootlegger with an evil reputation."*

Like Leatherdale, Plummer took Cuthbert's revelations to Gordon Scott but was told that Cuthbert had already made a confession on a confidential basis and so none of the information could be used against him. Scott maintained this was the position that had been taken by the Police Commission. Plummer said to Scott: "You have it now with no strings attached," and Scott said he would think about it.

The public listened in wonder and amazement as Plummer discussed the bookie conspiracy case of 1951, when he took his papers home for fear of information finding its way to the underworld. The detective testified he told then prosecutor Scott that he believed Mulligan and Cuthbert should be charged. Scott replied that the commission felt that what could be construed as "internal dissent" would be detrimental to the prosecution and could be interpreted as Plummer's jealousy of Mulligan. The case went down the drain, but it is interesting to consider what the outcome might have been if a full investigation had then been conducted into the Mulligan-Cuthbert racket. Plummer left the meeting with Scott an unhappy man. He told Tupper: "That is where it died and died right to this day."

On one occasion Tupper took a swipe at the media—a swipe that would not be quietly accepted today. The commissioner disliked a headline in the *Vancouver Herald* and told the paper's reporter to inform his editors that there were to be no more "large headlines." This was dictatorial and unusual even for that time, and Tupper added the ominous words: "If the press doesn't cooperate there are other means of handling that situation." The warning was ignored, and large headlines continued.

The *Herald* was a struggling, small-circulation morning paper, often money starved and frequently on the brink of folding. It landed in the glue again a few weeks later over another headline Tupper disliked. He summoned the publisher (Gerald M. Brown) and managing editor (Glyn Lewis) and extracted an apology. Their lawyer appeared and said the headline had occurred because the paper was short-staffed. The paper also published a statement apologizing for an "inexact" headline.

Next came the first of the Whelan brothers. This was the era of wide-brimmed fedoras, and they were much favoured by Jack Whelan, who brought a touch of *Guys and Dolls* to the hearing. Whelan, a stalky ex-wrestler with a face that reflected a lot of boisterous living, was a former detective who had put in 15 years on the force before quitting in 1946. He was the loose-cannon brother of Superintendent Harry Whelan. Mouthy and a braggart, he was a man whose ambitions far exceeded his abilities. Why he left the force was, at best, vaguely explained. Since then he had been a wrestling promoter, athletic club manager, truck driver, beer parlour waiter, news distributor, and private eye. One witness said Whelan at one time had wanted to become a bookie.

Whelan used a great deal of "street talk," and there was suspicion that Tupper was advertising his upper-crust status when he seemed not to understand this witness. Jack Whelan said a gambler had asked him to "fill me in." Tupper looked puzzled and asked, "Do you mean report to you?" When the spectators roared with laughter, Tupper again threatened to throw them all out. Whelan had been a detective-squad partner of Mulligan and had become the key source of much information fed to Munro, including the facts of a "piggy bank" caper exposed in *Flash*. Whelan and Mulligan were partners in 1945, when they went to investigate a West End break-in. While in the apartment, Whelan claimed Mulligan swiped a glass jar containing coins and hid it under his coat. Back in the cruiser, Whelan said Mulligan counted out the money and they split it, about $11 each. His descriptive style delighted the gallery, but his testimony rambled. He was not questioned closely about why he quit the force, but he maintained it was because of pressure from the Police Commission and the Athletic Commission—a licencing body for city sports events.

Whelan said: "I charged the Athletic Commission with aiding, abetting, condoning and perpetrating a scandal on the people of Vancouver." He complained nobody would listen to him.

Whelan told the inquiry that former alderman R.K. Gervin (Secretary of the Trades and Labour Council) and Bill Couper (who ran the Quadra Club) were involved in gambling in "the biggest, round-the-clock, round-the-calendar, sneak game."

Whelan darted from subject to subject but had the crowded courtroom hanging on every word as he related a story from 1949, when he was promoting wrestling. He was approached by long-time bookie Pete Wallace. A meeting followed, attended by Whelan, Cuthbert, Detective George Kitson, and the bookie. He testified that Wallace outlined a scheme for splitting up Vancouver gambling territory. Well known bookies Bruce Snider and Leo Bancroft would take all the territory west of Carroll Street, and everything else would belong to the four of them. Cuthbert would get $5,000 a month, but he said he wanted to check with Mulligan before deciding anything. Whelan drove Cuthbert to the police station. In a few minutes, Whelan said, Len came out of the building saying, "Everything is fixed." It was only day one of the inquiry, but already two respected cops and a savvy street rogue had implicated Vancouver's police chief.

Jack Whelan testified that in October 1954, eight months before the affair blew up, he met with city prosecutor Stewart McMorran in the Bamboo Terrace Restaurant and told his story. McMorran had taken over the prosecutor's office when Gordon Scott was appointed a magistrate in 1953. According to Whelan, "McMorran stated, 'There is enough evidence to blow this thing open,' and he wanted me to make a move but I said, 'I feel I want to go to bat

Edwin Percy "Pete" Wallace waits his turn to enter the inquiry and extol his innocence. Brothers Jack and Harry Whelan were a study in contrasts. Each commanded headlines for drastically different reasons.

for you but I don't want to catch your fly balls.'" Whelan's confusing metaphor provoked little action. Nothing happened until *Flash* hit the streets.

Whelan described another meeting in the *Province* boardroom in early 1955—a meeting attended by his brother Harry (the superintendent), Munro, and managing editor Bill Forst. Whelan told the inquiry his brother had told Forst that what Munro had on Mulligan was libelous, and it seems this scared the jittery *Province*, already unsure of the claims outlined by the mercurial Munro. Jack Whelan also maintained that the *Province* paid him $80 per week for his earlier private-eyeing for Munro. The paper later denied this.

Exactly how Jack Whelan and Ray Munro—both happy to pose for pictures during hearing breaks for the hordes of photographers who roamed the court house shooting almost everything that moved—got together was not spelled out at the inquiry. It was only disclosed that Munro frequented East End beer parlours and that Whelan slung beer at the Drake.

Whelan's testimony was an amazing and at times amusing mixture of tough-guy bombast and flowery rhetoric. He was critical of many, including Magistrate Oscar Orr: "He always seems to have a separate book of rules for senior officers." The *Province*'s Dan Ekman was delighted with the mixture of street lingo and such lyrical phrases as "from my storehouse of memories." Ekman also noted, in his daily gossip column, that if the inquiry went into late September it would be the longest downtown run since *Gone with the Wind*.

Before he left the stand, Whelan reinforced some imagery. He told Tupper that there had been death threats, including phone calls to his wife. "This is not kid stuff, this is rough stuff Munro and I are doing," said Whelan, adding, "I'm not afraid of anyone."

Detective George Kitson was called to the stand to testify concerning the proposition put to Jack Whelan and Len Cuthbert by the bookie Pete Wallace. He had been a member of the gambling squad for about four or five weeks when Cuthbert asked him to attend a meeting one Sunday morning in the York Hotel. Kitson said he was surprised to find Whelan at the meeting. He heard them discuss Wallace's scheme to carve up the gambling operation and open a bookie joint in the Dodson Hotel. Kitson claimed he later went to Cuthbert and said: "I don't know what you're talking about but from what I heard I don't want any part of it. I'm getting out." Kitson testified that after the meeting he went to see Gordon Scott and told him what he'd heard. Kitson then requested a transfer out of the gambling squad. His disclosure of the meeting with bookie Wallace was further evidence for the authorities of a police-bookie conspiracy. Kitson was the third policeman to go to city prosecutor Gordon Scott to seek action from the Police Commission regarding serious departmental problems, but still nothing happened.

The opening evidence given at the inquiry was sensational, as it related to bookie dealings and the connections between Mulligan, Cuthbert, and underworld rackets. Testimony from key witnesses—particularly Bob Leatherdale, Jack Whelan, and Archie Plummer—was explosive enough for Attorney General Robert Bonner to announce an RCMP probe of all "criminal aspects" cited. He stated that RCMP inspector M.J.Y. Dube from Regina, a 37-year-old cop with a law degree from the University of New Brunswick, would head the investigation, along with a sergeant and two constables from a BC detachment. Their probing went far and accounted for some of the inquiry's subsequent delays and adjournments. They even looked into possible jury tampering in previous bookie cases, but all their efforts were for nothing. Dube's final report to the Attorney General's Office either contained nothing of value or revealed too much. In any case, it was never released to the public and no recommendations based on its findings were ever made. Now it cannot be found, and so its contents remain a mystery.

Jack the-loose-cannon Whelan was followed on the stand by his brother Harry, the superintendent, who told of two dramatic sessions with Cuthbert, the first occurring on June 14 only 24 hours before *Flash* hit Vancouver streets with its exposé. Aware of what was to come in the tabloid, Harry Whelan asked Cuthbert to come to his office on the morning of June 14 because he had received some alarming information. Cuthbert replied that he also had some startling revelations to make. About their face-to-face encounter Whelan said: "I could see he was frightened, extremely agitated and extremely worried." When he arrived, Cuthbert told Whelan he had an 18-month-old son in addition to two daughters and was worried about being able to look after them if the graft was revealed, if he lost his job, or if he was sent to jail.

July 15, 2 days after Leatherdale and Plummer told their story, Robert Bonner (left) announced that the RCMP would investigate charges made during the probe. Inspector M.J.Y. Dube (right) was brought in from Regina to head up a four-man team.

Whelan asked Cuthbert if he was thinking of doing himself some harm, and the latter replied that he was considering some such move. "I warned him against taking any drastic action to harm himself," said Whelan, who had served on the force with Cuthbert for many years. "I told him I was aware of what had gone on and it wasn't a secret any more. I told Cuthbert I was not particularly concerned to see him get in trouble and I was familiar with the visit he was alleged to have made to Mayor Thompson some years ago. It was certainly common knowledge in the department."

Cuthbert said that he had first gone to see Scott "for the purpose of unburdening my soul" and that his statements at that time had been made in the strictest confidence. Whelan asked if he had received any proposition from Mulligan when he was appointed to head the gambling squad. The reply was: "The chief had told me I had to look after his friends. Any money received in payoffs was to be shared." Cuthbert stressed he was meticulous in giving half of what he took to Chief Mulligan.

Whelan continued his testimony regarding his meeting with Cuthbert. He wanted to know what Cuthbert knew about reports that Prosecutor McMorran had received—reports that suggested Jack Horton and Gordon Ambrose had been sent to Cuthbert by Mulligan in order to receive a share of the alleged payoffs. Cuthbert confirmed that these reports were "quite correct." When Whelan asked why he had made these disclosures, Cuthbert said he was afraid Mulligan was going to leave him holding the bag and he wanted some form of protection. He left Whelan's office after a 20-minute meeting.

Whelan made notes of the conversation and, next day, June 15, gave a copy of them to Stewart McMorran. That same day *Flash* carried Ray Munro's sensational stories. The local media were caught off guard and were uncertain what to do. Reporters harried the police commissioners but were consistently told that the latter had no comment, except to say that the allegations were being investigated. This went on until the fateful days of June 23 and 24. Whelan told the inquiry that on June 23 McMorran phoned his office and said he wanted to see Cuthbert immediately. The detective sergeant was contacted and agreed to come in the next day.

Early next morning Harry Whelan told the inquiry: "I gave [Cuthbert] a copy of my notes and he appeared to be surprised at the extent of them." Asked to sign the notes, Cuthbert questioned the ramifications of signing or not signing: "I told him he was stuck in the middle and it was best for him to line himself up on the side of law and order." Cuthbert agreed with everything "but he demurred on one point. He didn't want to get his men in trouble and wanted to delete the words 'I was to take care of the men.'"

Cuthbert left the meeting, went downstairs to the squad room, asked the lone occupant to get him a cup of coffee, sat down, and within minutes shot himself. When he heard the shot ring out, Whelan knew immediately what Cuthbert had done. As the wounded man was being wheeled out on a gurney, Whelan rushed out, leaned over, and asked: "No hard feelings, I hope?" Cuthbert whispered back: "No hard feelings." It was a bizarre scene that puzzled reporters who were unaware of the dramatic meeting that had taken place only minutes before.

When Whelan presented his notes as exhibits, Mulligan's lawyer and other counsel complained, claiming that Cuthbert's state of mind had to be taken into account. There were suggestions that Cuthbert had been pressured by Whelan into making and signing the statement and that his mental condition could have been affected. Tupper disagreed, saying that a psychiatrist's report on Cuthbert was made after the shooting. Whelan's testimony was put over for cross-examination at a later date, but, tragically, it was never to be.

In the meantime, another player in the drama took centre stage. Identified by Jack Whelan in his evidence as a leading gambler, Pete Wallace told the *Sun* in an interview that he was actually only a "two-bit bookie." The 47-year-old millwright complained: "They talk like I am a real big shot, a sort of Al Capone but I'm only a two-bit bookie who never had $5,000 at one time." Wallace had lost count of the number of times he had been arrested, noting that Leatherdale was the last to nick him. He said he had given up the bookie racket five years earlier and had gone to work in a mill because his kids were reading in the papers about his run-ins with the law. When he took the stand Wallace denied everything, saying he never met Cuthbert or gave him bribery money or made any other payments to the police. He intrigued the audience when he produced two old tattered $100 cheques stamped NSF. He said he got them from Jack Whelan as payment for a loan.

George Sutherland, identified by Cuthbert as one of those who delivered brown bags full of bribe money, denied the allegation just as Wallace had done. He admitted, however, that he was a bookie and had operated a chain of gambling outlets.

Webster's audience was growing, Munro was as cocky as ever, and the major dailies were giving the inquiry massive coverage in order to make up for earlier omissions. There was one voice all were waiting to hear.

While everybody waited for Len Cuthbert's testimony, he was recovering from his bullet wound at Vancouver General Hospital. Cuthbert was 54 and had been a policeman since 1926 His wife was a nurse, and they had a young family: an 18-month-old son and two older adopted daughters, 12 and 16, respectively. *Province* reporter Ed Moyer, the man with the best police contacts in town, was the first to see Cuthbert in hospital. Moyer found him at his hobby, making slippers out of pieces of sheepskin. They talked about everything except the probe. A *Province* staff photographer took a photo of a very frail Cuthbert. Len had never been a particularly robust man, and recent events had obviously taken a heavy toll.

The bullet Cuthbert fired into his own chest missed his heart but tore through his body and slammed into the ante-room wall behind him. The first two policemen who rushed to his aid found him slumped in a chair semi-conscious. He told them: "I tried to get my heart. I'm sorry I missed." Police doctor K.L. Panton said immediately after the shooting: "He should be dead, I can't understand why he isn't."

The inquiry received regular reports on Cuthbert's condition and his fitness to testify. Tupper had gone to the hospital on July 2 to speak personally with the policeman in order to establish when he might be ready to testify. Cuthbert's colleagues said he had been distraught since *Flash*'s stories began to appear in mid-June. At times he was almost at the point of hysteria. He couldn't eat, and pounds seemed to fall from him. Mulligan's lawyer demanded an independent psychiatric assessment after the inquiry was told by one doctor that Cuthbert was extremely confused but sane. Cuthbert's lawyer was not opposed to Norris's request but insisted: "I am not willing to turn my client into a guinea pig for all the psychiatrists in Vancouver." Tupper, who was of the old school, offered his own views of psychiatrists: "I will tell the Vancouver General Hospital that so far as I am concerned I have no objection to a whole cloud of psychiatrists going in to see him." He believed he could tell "an idiot" if he saw one in the box as well as could any psychiatrist. The media reported that sources close to Cuthbert maintained he would tell all when he was in the witness box. There was no chance, they said, that he would again try to kill himself because he had "talked" to his 18-month-old son.

Cuthbert had been less than discreet about his activities. Inspector John Dunn was another witness who had heard the story. He recalled Cuthbert telling him that Deputy Chief Gordon Ambrose was a good friend of Celona and was involved in a payoff. Dunn was astonished when Cuthbert said he would like this information passed to the prosecutor. Dunn gave the information to Scott, by then a judge, when McMorran was with him. "They made no comment and I dropped the matter," he said. It was a story that both Scott and McMorran had heard before.

The inquiry was not without its amusing diversions. The news media gave coverage to a visit by Montreal mayor Jean Drapeau, who, as a battling prosecutor, had helped fight crime in his own city and police department. Drapeau opined that a department needed a chief with integrity— one who set high standards and demanded the best of his men. While implying that he had fared better than most, he said a crime clean-up could not take place overnight. Ironically, this was substantiated by a wire news report from Montreal shortly after Drapeau arrived in Vancouver. It stated that 30 cops had raided a blind pig following shootings and violence at four Montreal nightclubs.

Known as Montreal's new crime buster, 39-year-old Mayor Jean Drapeau stayed out of Vancouver politics, saying "the mayor of one city does not talk about the affairs of another."

Vancouverites chuckled and then got back to their real concern: When were they going to hear from Len Cuthbert?

Despondent and confused, Len Cuthbert was the father of three when he attempted suicide. Earlier confessions of his crimes fell on deaf ears and apparently failed to relieve his inner burden. Nobody offered him penance or absolution.

8.　Cuthbert Testifies

If he is insane he is dangerous, but I don't think he is insane he is merely a psychopath and as such is responsible for his actions.

Lawyer Tom Norris describes Ray Munro

When the news broke that Cuthbert would take the stand on July 28, public excitement peaked. Lawyers and reporters who knew they had seats in the relatively small courtroom relaxed over coffee across the street in the old Devonshire and Georgia Hotels. It was different for members of the public who were eager to watch the scandal first hand. Crowds started gathering on the court house steps hours before the 11:00 a.m. start. When the doors opened would-be spectators elbowed each other in a race through the halls to get a ringside view. Again, the fire marshal said enough was enough and moved many outside. As expected the press table was jam-packed. The most senior and experienced newsmen in town were on the prowl outside and in the corridors to pick up any angles they could find. British-trained reporters Paddy Sherman and Jack Brooks could match Webster's shorthand and were to fill column after column for the *Province*. Columnists Jack Wasserman and Dan Ekman saw it as a new and gushing source for their gossip columns. Veteran sob-sister Simma Holt was on the scene. Vancouver was poised for big news and it wasn't disappointed. Again it was hot and muggy. In the courtroom the temperature soared. The scene was set for Act I of a tragedy. The key players were in place.

Len Cuthbert, born in 1901, joined the force in 1925, two years before Mulligan. He was a special constable attached to what was then the dry squad, the liquor law enforcement group. He became a regular a year later and was a beat cop. In 1935 Cuthbert was badly injured in a waterfront labour dispute at Ballantine Pier. As the *Province* reported in April 1935: "During the riot one of the most severely injured among the police was Constable Len Cuthbert. He was dragged from an automobile in a lane near

Heatley Avenue by nearly a dozen men. They used an axe to smash the car in which he was travelling alone. He was kicked, pounded and stoned. When he was picked up a large blood-spattered stone was lying beside him. He was unconscious." Cuthbert was taken to hospital and recovered from his injuries. He was promoted to detective along with his pal Mulligan in 1937. He was demoted once for an infraction, but his career, on the surface, was steady if unspectacular.

Cuthbert's lawyer, H.A.D. Oliver, commonly known as "Had," was a character in his own right, one of many stars the probe produced—and one who never eschewed publicity. Oliver resembled some of the personalities from the British *Rumpole* television series about the Old Bailey: the Eton-Oxford-Cambridge-educated, bowler-hatted, urbane, polished, and confident members of the establishment. He first arrived in Vancouver from England in 1951, a 31-year-old bachelor and an economist and a lawyer. During his visit Oliver told reporters he was looking for industrial opportunities. He returned the next year to take up residence. The Bentley he drove gave the press the impression he was "the model of an English barrister," and he soon became a prominent Vancouver lawyer. During the probe Oliver remarked to Tupper: "It has been said the only difference between people in prison and people out of prison is that the ones in prison have been found out."

Before Cuthbert entered the room lawyers gave what amounted to opening statements. Oliver told the hearing: "I would ask you to remember this man, who a few weeks ago was at death's door, has come from his hospital bed to testify and will return there." Oliver emphasized that Cuthbert had a strong sense of loyalty to the men he worked with but had only a limited amount of strength to do what he knew must be done. Commissioner Tupper pointed out that Cuthbert must undergo "vigorous and full examination." That phrase aptly described the approach of Mulligan's lawyer Tom Norris, who commented that Cuthbert's state of mind would be determined during the hearing.

Tall, burly, and leather-lunged, Norris had a fine command of the English language, again in the style of the fictional *Rumpole*. *Province* reporter Jean Haworth wrote that Norris's "Toby Jug face" would switch from a smile to a scowl in a split second. Unlike Rumpole, however, Norris was an elitist, a well-endowed member of Vancouver's legal fraternity. In further contrast, Norris had both a liking and a respect for the best drink in the house, while Rumpole made do with Chateau Thames Embankment plonk. Norris was admitted to the bar in 1919. A native of Victoria, he had served as an artillery officer in the First World War and as a deputy advocate general and Canadian legal adviser to the famous General Bernard "Monty" Montgomery in the Second World War.

Norris had a few things to get off his chest and, brushing aside the niceties, he rose to his feet to launch, in Mulligan's defence, a blistering attack that had reporters scurrying for the phones and sure-fire headlines. In top form, relishing the moment, Norris let fly. His voice rose and fell, booming and then almost whispering the tirade that ranged from slashing invective to humourous cajolery. It was vintage Norris who attacked Munro. "If he is insane he is dangerous, but I don't think he is insane he is merely a psychopath and as such is responsible for his actions." Munro sat smiling as Norris hacked and slashed. Munro's lawyer, Neil Fleishman, complained bitterly about the insane comment, but the onslaught went on. Norris barely paused for breath, his face growing red.

Norris asked Tupper for a contempt order against *Flash*, its editor, and Munro. He launched a lengthy attack, flaying them for publishing libelous and scurrilous articles against a background of "filth and obscenity." The lawyer thundered that there had recently been a "most objectionable" editorial in *Flash* and the promise by the Toronto editors that they wouldn't publish others like it wasn't enough. The audience laughed and appreciated Norris's performance when he noted that some felt a good old-fashioned horsewhipping was the proper method of dealing with such people, but, of course, he was not going to comment on this.

Holding copies of the latest *Flash* headlines like pieces of used toilet paper, Norris had the public galleries howling when, in stentorian tones, he read "Chicken Press Helps Crooks Win Vancouver" and "Get With It— Mulligan Should Be Behind Bars." The piece maintained that the crooks knew the cops' every move. Munro laughed with the spectators, but Mulligan didn't find it funny. Tupper took the contempt request under advisement but later disallowed it.

Then it was time for what the public had come to see. The gallery leaned forward for the best possible look as a frail, wan Cuthbert came in, a nurse at his side (whom Norris claimed was mere window dressing). Cuthbert carefully made his way to the box. For the swearing in he clutched the bible in both hands. Then began five days of examination, gently led by Cuthbert's lawyer H.A.D. Oliver. This was followed by Norris's blistering cross-examination.

Sun reporters jumped at the chance for great copy and, in the best tabloid style, churned out some colourful prose. Readers learned Cuthbert looked "waxy under the harsh Assize Court lights, visibly trying to make peace with his conscience . . . before a mob of thrusting, scuffling, hissing spectators as he clutched his breast where earlier he had shot himself, rocking back and forth like a caged animal and insisting his chief must share his guilt." It was great stuff, right off the grocery store magazine rack. Nobody could remember any scuffling or hissing, but the word-pictures went on: "While a muggy

In 1955 Vancouver's competing papers had different styles. On July 28/29 the Sun *tititllated with garish headlines while maintaining a profile for the racetrack crowd. The* Province's *approach was more sedate.*

draught came off Georgia Street, stirring the rust-coloured drapes in the high courtroom windows, the professional policeman picked at the fabric of his memory unravelling the tortured story." Readers were told that reporters knew Cuthbert as a "brick-wall of a man" but that now little more than a shell remained.

Cuthbert certainly looked awful, and at times he swayed from side to side on the stand. At the first recess he told a reporter he doubted he could go on much longer. There was, however, to be much more for Cuthbert in the form of a relentless, almost brutal, cross-examination by Norris.

Oliver told the hearing that his client would admit "improperly accepting certain sums of money after 23 years of loyal service in the police department." He stated the graft had taken place over a short six-week period six years earlier. At first Oliver led his client gently through the details of his life on the force and the sequence of events that shattered a long and, to that time, relatively fault-free career. Cuthbert admitted he had gone up the ladder because of his relationship with Mulligan. Their friendship had developed over the years, as Mulligan learned that Cuthbert could be dominated and would always obey orders. Now Cuthbert was paying the price.

Speaking very slowly, Cuthbert explained how he met Mulligan in the hallway at the police station in 1948. The chief offered him a job as the detective sergeant in charge of the gambling squad, and he jumped at the chance: "Mulligan said I would have to follow his instructions and do what I was told. He also said in one form or another that the gambling squad job

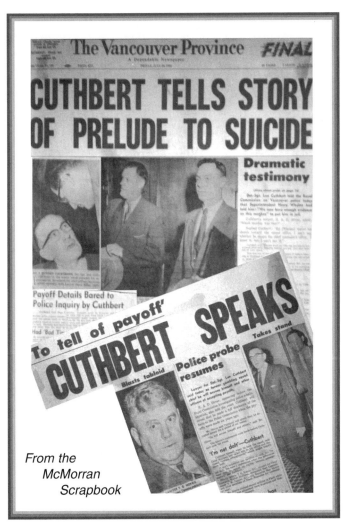

*From the
McMorran
Scrapbook*

was a good job and that there were certain arrangements which could possibly be made whereby we would materially benefit. I don't think he said money, as far as money or cash, but I am not dumb I think I drew the correct inference when I deduced that he meant money."

Cuthbert's initial admission covered only a brief time span. After he got the job, he and Mulligan shared up to four $500 payments from bookie Pete Wallace and $300 from a man named Sutherland. The payments from Wallace were made at intervals of about 10 days. Cuthbert and Wallace would meet near the Canadian National Railways station, off Main Street, where Wallace would deliver a paper bag containing money and one or two bottles of whisky. Cuthbert kept the liquor for himself and took the money to Mulligan, at which time they would split it in half.

No one listened more intently to Cuthbert's confessions than did the off-duty policemen seated in the galleries. Cuthbert contended he kept half of his share of the loot and split the rest with other members in the gambling squad. There were audible sounds of disbelief from the spectators, however, when Cuthbert testified that he couldn't remember exactly who on the squad got money, as personnel were rotated frequently.

Mulligan continued to take notes as his former partner in graft spoke. Cuthbert said he well knew that criminal charges could be laid against him. He also recalled that Wallace had had control of the bookie business in the East End during the time in question and had wanted to add a book in the 100-block East Hastings. Cuthbert said Wallace had offered to pay $5,000 to the cops if they would allow him to operate freely in this area.

Under Oliver's questioning Cuthbert said that, in 1949, he met with Prosecutor Gordon Scott and unburdened himself about the payoffs. Scott then took Cuthbert to Mayor Charles Thompson's home, where he repeated his story and asked to be transferred out of the gambling squad. Although transfers were normally made at the recommendation of the chief, this one appears to have been initiated by the Police Commission. Did Mulligan and Cuthbert have a falling out? Did the commission transfer Cuthbert to clerical duties and then tell Mulligan it had done so? None of this was ever explained during the hearings. Another major point never pursued was why the payoffs ended. Cuthbert said they stopped, but why? What made him confess to Scott? Was he scared of being caught or had he and Mulligan had a disagreement? Did Mulligan sense Cuthbert had been a bad choice and change bagmen? The questions were never asked, and so they were never answered.

When questions turned to current events, Cuthbert testified that, about June 9 or 10 Munro came to his house on West Twenty-Third Avenue, while Jack Whelan sat outside in a car. Munro pulled out a gun and told him: "You are in trouble. You have got one of three choices. You can blow your brains out, or you can go to jail, or you can see the right party." This third option involved swearing an affidavit regarding his participation in departmental graft for Munro's lawyer, Neil Fleishman. Munro's words obviously had a serious impact on Cuthbert, who repeated them as though they had been burned into his brain.

After Munro left, Cuthbert went to the home of Judge Gordon Scott, to whom he had told his story in 1949 when Scott was a city prosecutor, and informed him it was no longer "a secret." Scott told him to await developments. The bomb-shell hit the streets June 15 in the pages of *Flash*.

Most of the time the courtroom was quiet as a tomb because Cuthbert dropped his voice at crucial moments, and it was hard to hear at the back of the chamber. The members of the assembly leaned forward in their seats, straining for every word.

H.A.D. Oliver, Len Cuthbert's lawyer, holding documents, discusses a point with a glum-faced Tom Norris (Mulligan's lawyer) and his associate.

Cuthbert described June 24 as "a day I will never forget." He had gone to Whelan's office shortly after arriving at the station about 7.45 a.m. Chewing on his thumb at times, and with his lips trembling, Cuthbert said: "I had already decided to shoot myself." He told of discussing the crisis with Whelan and signing the statement. Cuthbert said Whelan attacked Mulligan during their meeting, stating: "Imagine the cheapskate and other disparaging remarks . . . and he said imagine him making you pay the boys out of your share." Cuthbert left Whelan and went back to the ante-room off the squad room, where he asked a colleague to get some coffee. Then he took his service revolver, pointed it at his chest, and pulled the trigger.

Obviously in distress while giving much of this evidence, Cuthbert was at other times almost jaunty. Wasserman reported that, during a recess, he had quipped to a friend that he could lick his weight in wildcats "provided they were tied down." He needed every ounce of inner strength he possessed for what came next—cross-examination by Norris.

Mulligan's lawyer, by his size and bulk alone, dominated the front of the courtroom. Norris was in his element as the challenger. He was Norris the tenacious, Norris the performer, aware of the attention he commanded and the audience that was his alone. There was no jury, but there was a huge assembly of the public, the press, and his peers. He mounted the attack. Pointing at Cuthbert, he accused him of "living a fraud and a lie as a policeman" and of issuing a "tissue of falsehoods." Cuthbert blanched and looked shaken at the lawyer's opening accusations, but he surprised the room by hitting back. When Norris said he could prove all these accusations, Cuthbert answered: "That will take some proving."

Norris traced Cuthbert's career from 1925, when he joined the force on a part-time basis. With all the scorn he could muster, Norris charged that

Cuthbert had become part of a conspiracy to destroy Mulligan, "a man the whole underworld fears. You became a tool of officers who had a grudge against the chief and other senior officers the chief had disciplined or had passed over in promotion."

Bruised by the assault, Cuthbert asked for a break and Tupper granted it. One reporter said he was unsteady on his feet when he came back, walking very gingerly, "as though his bones were made of chalk." Cuthbert admitted he had accepted bribes over a three-and-a-half-month period and not just for six weeks, as he had stated earlier. The witness acknowledged he was no "purist" and, before the deal with Mulligan, had at Christmas accepted a tie or a pair of socks or the odd bottle from various people. He told Norris that under his arrangement with the chief he had received about $1,150.

The spectators chuckled at one exchange that got too close to the lawyer's heart. Cuthbert said that, prior to the bookies' bribes, "I might have had the odd bottle of whisky given to me."

Norris: "From whom did you receive the liquor?"

Cuthbert: "I have received liquor from barristers . . . "

Norris: "Oh I don't mean . . .

Cuthbert: " . . . and other respectable citizens. That could be called a bribe if you wanted to get technical about it."

Norris didn't and moved on.

Cuthbert got a small grain of satisfaction and another opportunity to needle Norris when he quoted Mulligan as saying that, if they got into trouble, he would hire "the best lawyers in Eastern Canada to fight it." Norris bristled, as was expected, and demanded: "Did he say he would hire the best lawyers in Eastern Canada to fight it to a standstill? And why the East?"

Savouring the brief moment, Cuthbert paused and replied: "I think he said, he'd get better talent there." Appreciating that he'd been had, Norris allowed a small smile and admitted: "That's what I expected."

The *Sun*'s banner headline described the next major turn of events. It read: "Cuthbert Refuses to Name the Gambling Squad Men He Split Money with Six Years Ago." Cuthbert's testimony started to ramble during a bitter attack from Norris, who stalked the room shouting out his questions. Becoming noticeably worried and uncertain, Cuthbert at times faltered under the barrage. "You are not going to get those names out of me," he told Norris. "I am not going to hurt anyone else." The lawyer charged he had no hesitation in hurting Deputy Chief Gordon Ambrose and Superintendent Jack Horton, but Cuthbert stated: "I have certainly no desire to hurt the men under my direction."

Norris's assault moved into a second day and then a third. He showed Cuthbert a list of 12 men who had been in the detail at that time. Looking as

From the
McMorran
Scrapbook

Tupper demanded that Cuthbert identify corruption amongst his men. Depicted as frail and easily led by his many critics, Cuthbert stood firm in his resistance.

though he was ready to crumble, Cuthbert said he hadn't meant the whole squad had been in on the money split. This was a key point. In a witness room just outside the main courtroom, members of his squad were waiting to testify. Tupper stepped in and warned Cuthbert about perjury, adding he would give "very little attention" to his evidence against Mulligan if he didn't tell all.

One of the many lawyers in court, Lyle Jestley, who represented Jack Horton, interjected and told Cuthbert that squad members would be called to deny his claim that they shared the bribe money. However, Cuthbert hung tough. Norris read out the names of the squad members, stating that by not naming names Cuthbert was "putting a whole body of these men under some cloud." Cuthbert replied: "I would hurt them a lot more if I pointed the finger at the wrong men." Answering Tupper, he added: "I cannot with any positive degree of certainty swear that any of these men on the list received money from me." He said it was obvious his memory had been better when he talked to Bob Leatherdale six years earlier. Cuthbert later gave Tupper the names of four members of the squad whom he said he was sure didn't share in any bribes. They were James Frew, Dick Harrison, Tom Stokes, and John McHardy.

For Cuthbert, the hours spent in the witness box over five days tore his life apart. He said he had enjoyed one "period of prosperity," when his mother had left him about $5,000 in her estate. Asked when this was he nervously counted off months on his fingers. Under Norris's relentless questioning, he admitted being demoted from detective to constable for trying to seduce a woman in a case he was investigating. He said he had also once been suspended for supplying bootleg liquor to fellow members at the station. A bizarre incident was described, in which Cuthbert arrived at the police station drunk. Norris claimed Cuthbert's career had been troubled by money, women, and whisky. Questioned about the woman involved, a weary Cuthbert remained defiant, saying to Norris: "You can't hurt me any more, read it and I will tell you if it's true." Norris cast more doubt on the witness's credibility when he got him to admit he had bought a house from Rose Capello, a well-known bootlegger. He bought the house at 16th and Cambie for $4,000 ($350 down and $35 a month). (Tupper's report later concluded that Cuthbert had paid full market value and purchased the house through a real estate agent.)

One relationship that had the press and the public curious was never explained. Cuthbert denied saying that Mulligan was close to former attorney general Gordon Wismer. The galleries listened intently as he stated that Mulligan "had a happy knack of getting along with people and making friends."

Norris pointed to inconsistencies in Cuthbert's evidence and asked: "Having that in mind how far can you suggest the rest of your evidence can be relied on?" Cuthbert replied: "That is for the commissioner to decide."

Jack Horton's lawyer, Lyle Jestley, was the next one to take on the cross-examination of Cuthbert, asking him to name bookie joints he had protected. Cuthbert got caught when he said he knew only about 10 bookies. Jestley immediately pointed out that Cuthbert had registered some 100 convictions during his gambling squad tenure. Cuthbert then admitted that he "must have been mistaken." He also admitted to Jestley that he was wrong when he said he had not read any accounts of the inquiry prior to taking the stand. Jestley's cross-examination was in sharp contrast to Norris's. He talked to Cuthbert in quiet, almost fatherly tones and received a very emotional response. At times Cuthbert had trouble speaking. He wiped tears from his eyes with the back of his hand, and his head slumped onto his chest.

Cuthbert's ordeal finally came to an end after gruelling days that sapped the energy of a man who, after all, had recently tried to commit suicide and was still suffering the physical and psychological effects of this. Many found it difficult not to feel sympathy for him, despite his admissions.

Thousands continued to listen to Webster's nightly broadcasts. His heavy Scottish accent intrigued many, particularly when he altered his voice to mimic witnesses, although one man grumpily told a reporter he didn't listen because he couldn't stand foreign-language broadcasts.

As the headlines grew, Tupper expressed his amazement at the public interest and the widening web of involvement the testimony was creating. He felt the whole business was "distasteful for everybody." Response to the interest in this inquiry included an unusual letter from George Shea, secretary of the Chief Constables Association of Canada. It was written in extravagant language and supported Mulligan, who was a former president of the association. Shea maintained that no one had been a better president than Mulligan and that there was a nefarious scheme to destroy him. "We believe that evil forces, including some jealous and disloyal members of the force have unjustly and maliciously attempted to have the chief removed from office. It is our view that no scoundrel is as low as a police officer who is unfaithful to his trust and who uses his position as a cloak to shield his putrescence." Shea's view seemed to be largely his own, however, as the association spent some time dissociating itself from his tirade.

The *Province*'s Dan Ekman noted that public distaste for what the inquiry was uncovering was obviously shared by some people who had thought of becoming police officers. Between April and August 86 applicants were judged eligible for jobs on the Vancouver police force. However, only 43 of the 70 expected showed up. According to Ekman, more than a few people had a chuckle when Hollywood star Cary Grant came to town to plug his new movie, *To Catch a Thief*.

Reporters chased principal witnesses both inside and outside the courtroom. One who went to Cuthbert's house managed a brief interview. In a trembling voice, and speaking through a closed door, the detective said: "Everybody is suffering, my family, everybody. I cannot sleep, but I want to keep away from sleeping pills."

When the inquiry took a day off, reporters looked elsewhere for angles. There was a minor embarrassment for the police when Acting Chief Alan Rossiter was forced to explain buying a TV set from W.C. Mainwaring, President of BC Electric (forerunner of BC Hydro). Rossiter told the probe he learned of the available television from a BCE public relations man. This caused a lot of eye-rolling in the gallery thanks to mounting suspicions concerning all members of the force. Rossiter produced a cancelled $250 cheque and hotly denied that BCE got a break on parking tickets. Insult was added to injury when a TV technician testified that Rossiter paid too much and that the set was worth only $139.50.

Then the inquiry was back in session, with yet more unexpected developments.

From the McMorran Scrapbook

The Vancouver Sun

Sup't Whelan Shot in Heart

TOP COP KILLS SELF

Decision Reserved On Contempt Count

Action Hangs on Fine Legal Point, Commissioner Tupper Declares

Contempt 'Serious One'

Journal Has Less

MARGARET'S DECISION ON WEDDING PLANS DUE

Due Today To Testify

DIES OF SELF-INFLICTED WOUND

The Vancouver Herald

Western Canada's Largest Morning Newspaper

WHELAN FEARED REVIV' OF OLD FAMILY TRAGED'

Fleishman Recalls Ta' In Police HQ Corrid'

Parsloe Report Branded $1700 Pot Of Whitewash

The Vancouver Province
A Dependable Newspaper

SECRET PROBE CLEARED CHIEF MULLIGAN IN '50

Ex-mayor on stand

"There is not the slightest semblance of truth in the assertion that Chief Mulligan is engaged in anything illegal."

That was the dramatic statement read to the Tupper police probe today.

Supt. Whelan kills self with gun

Henry Whelan shoots self at his home

LAWYER CLAIMS WHELAN FACED 'INSANITY SMEAR'

The Vancouver Sun

RCMP. Say 'Just Rumor'

9.   Popular Policeman Dies

When I die my kids will not be ashamed of me. Nobody will
have cause to tell them your father was a crook.
                              Superintendent Harry Whelan

Three hours before he was due to take the stand again, Harry Whelan
committed suicide. On the morning of August fifth the headlines read: "Police
Superintendent Kills Self." Radio stations broke into regular programming
with the tragic news. Whelan, like Cuthbert before him, pointed a .38 revolver
at his chest and pulled the trigger. Whelan didn't miss. The public was to
learn later that he died in the same room and used the same gun his father had
used to do the same deed. He had also suffered through his only daughter's
suicide. His widow said he had been unable to sleep, got out of bed, and went
into the living room. She rushed to his side after hearing the shot, but there
was nothing she could do.

Whelan's suicide rocked the Tupper Inquiry. His death added to
speculation and suspicion. There had been nothing to implicate him directly
in graft, and when the probe was over no finger was ever pointed at him.
There was no doubt, however, that Whelan disliked Mulligan and felt he was
destroying the force. The animosity between the two had intensified since
September 1953. Whelan had risen to the position of assistant police chief
but was demoted by Mulligan following a brawl at a police social event at the
Peace Portal Golf Course. On the way home Whelan's car was stopped at the
Pattulo Bridge by the RCMP, who suspected him of drunk driving. Mulligan
came down hard on his deputy, calling his involvement in these two events a
major breach of conduct. Mulligan said a reprimand was insufficient
punishment and demoted the assistant chief two grades to junior
superintendent. Whelan never forgot. He protested that the punishment was
too severe and maintained the Peace Portal hassle and his subsequent driving
problem arose because he lost his temper, not because he was drunk.

Whelan was 53 and had been a policeman since 1927; he was one of the
department's most popular senior officers and went calmly and competently

about his work. He had been to sea as a boy and got his mariner's ticket at the age of 21. He was the youngest skipper on the West Coast before he joined the force. While committed to his job, Whelan was not obsessed by it. Regarding his occupation, the papers said he told friends: "It's a job." He was also quoted as stating: "When I die my kids will not be ashamed of me. Nobody will have cause to tell them your father was a crook." In his private life he enjoyed fishing with a barber friend and taking two teenaged sons to watch the police softball team. A few weeks after his death, when the Police Mutual Benevolent Association Team won the BC Senior Men's League championship, team captain Dip Smith told reporters: "We won it for Harry." Team members were among the hundreds who attended Whelan's funeral, where there was a great outpouring of sincere emotion and sorrow.

Attorney General Robert Bonner stepped in and announced he had asked the RCMP to expand their investigation to include Whelan's death. Superintendent George Archer, head of the RCMP's BC detachment, commented: "This is certainly a most unusual request but it appears we are living in unusual times."

The inquest into Whelan's death was held in mid-August before Coroner Glen McDonald. Special investigator RCMP sergeant John Knox testified he was present when Whelan's safety deposit box was opened. The Mountie looked through all Whelan's personal papers and found nothing detrimental. Knox testified that, in his opinion, it was a suicide with no other involvements.

Whelan's widow told the inquest jury her husband had been distressed since the probe began. He was not concerned about himself but about some of the evidence he would have to give. He worried that his erratic brother Jack was in a tough spot. Mrs. Whelan cried as she told the inquest: "He didn't take a nickel from anybody." They still had the same furniture they bought when they were married. Regardless, Mrs. Whelan said Harry told her: "They will blame me for everything."

Evidence given at the Whelan inquest by Munro's lawyer Neil Fleishman threw new light on events. Fleishman was another colourful member of Vancouver's legal fraternity. A graduate of UBC, he went to sea as a stoker before joining the army in the Second World War. He studied law and received his degree in 1948, before articling with his father's firm.

Described in *The Advocate* as "flamboyant and a bit noisy," Fleishman's green waistcoat was one of his hallmarks. He was a cigar-smoking lover of classical music and a good violinist. Most of his legal life was spent in divorce and family court. He also wrote a number of books, including an autobiography entitled *Counsel for the Damned*.

Fleishman told the inquest that he met Whelan by chance a short time before the latter's suicide, during a visit to the station. In conversation he told an obviously worried Whelan to expect a lengthy, in-depth cross-examination, which would include revealing details about his personal life. Fleishman suggested Mulligan had acquired information about the Whelan brothers and would try to have them declared insane. This was later declared untrue by Sergeant Knox, who said it was nothing more than rumour—its source being a divorce lawyer who worked the East End and did some of his own sleuthing.

Flamboyant Neil Montefiore Fleishman (centre) and his bookends Ray Munro (right) and Jack Whelan (left) were inseparable during the early days of the trial.

Fleishman shocked the inquest as he recounted the conversation he had had with Whelan two days before the tragic suicide. He said Superintendent Whelan asked him: "What are they going to do to me?

"I said, 'I guess they are going to give you a going over about your daughter.'

"He said, 'I can't live through her tragedy again. Do they know about my father?,

"I said, 'What about your father?'

"He said, 'He committed suicide.'

"I said, 'My god, I didn't know that,' and he looked very upset and walked out to the car park and that was the last time I saw him."

It took the inquest jury only 20 minutes to return a verdict. It ruled Whelan's death "unnatural . . . the result of a self-inflicted gun shot wound … this resulting from recent extreme mental strain."

When the probe resumed Fleishman was rapped sharply by Tupper—"severely castigated," as the papers reported—for behaving unprofessionally in talking to Whelan. An angry Tupper said that at his hearing there would be "no smear campaign against private lives and no one must fear giving testimony." He asked Fleishman to express regret to the court for his conduct. After the apology, Fleishman added: "My statement was [meant] to steel him and I thought it was quite proper."

Fleishman later complained that his ethics and integrity had been impugned by Tupper's criticism of his conduct. The lawyer said he was obeying a moral duty to a friend, "and for that I can express no regrets."

10.   Norris vs The Union

You're babysitting big hulking police officers.

Tom Norris

When the probe resumed in early September it was Norris who again took centre stage. He listened to a group of policemen whose testimony resulted in further revelations about Mulligan's administration. Most of the grievances, which were about promotion and seniority, had been orchestrated by the police union. The union's real driving force was secretary Dan Brown, labelled a union man "first, last, and always." This was abundantly clear when Brown disagreed on the stand with union president Ed Dougherty's earlier statement that Mulligan had "great executive ability." The police union was a major muscle-flexer and had opposed and disliked Mulligan from that day in 1947 when he leapfrogged over many senior officers to become top cop.

A pensive Tom Norris sits in an empty courtroom pondering a question from Vancouver Sun *reporter Simma Holt. In early September 1955 he was a man with much on his mind.*

Norris relished taking on Dougherty and Brown. He charged them with "babysitting big hulking police officers" who should have been ashamed and embarrassed to testify, with their "tuppenny, ha'penny" complaints. He had the gallery roaring, and even Tupper smiled and didn't threaten to clear the room when old soldier Norris quoted a favourite Second World War ditty: "Kiss me goodnight sergeant-major, tuck me in my little wooden bed … we all love you sergeant-major, sergeant major be a mother to me." Spectators loved it; union leaders were less amused.

Norris chided some of the police witnesses for mumbling on the stand. He asked Tupper to get them to speak up, maintaining they were talking "as if they were speaking to their best girl from behind a rose bush."

Bombshells were nothing new at the probe, but on September 8, as the inquiry was preparing for a change of venue, Tom Norris dropped one that took everyone by surprise. He quit. Later it was learned that Tupper knew

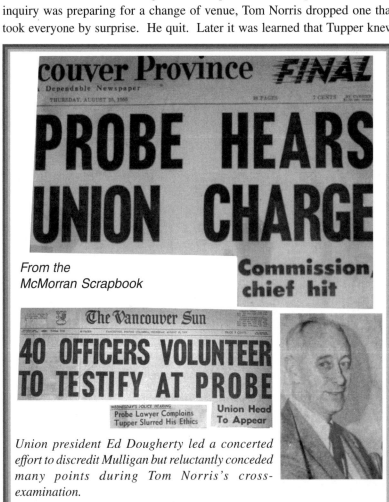

From the
McMorran Scrapbook

Union president Ed Dougherty led a concerted effort to discredit Mulligan but reluctantly conceded many points during Tom Norris's cross-examination.

this was coming. but lawyers, police, the press, and spectators were puzzled by this latest twist. Mulligan also claimed to have been surprised by the move but was seemingly unruffled as he and Norris left the hearing smiling and arm-in-arm. There had been rumours that Norris was in line for a judgeship, but he declined reporters' questions and gave nothing away. He said that under normal circumstances he would not have issued a statement, "but I consider it proper to state my confidence in the chief, in the truth of my client's case as it will be developed and to emphasize that my reason for withdrawing was entirely personal and has nothing to do with any projected evidence against the chief constable which could be at all relevant to this inquiry and of which I have had particulars." The media went on the hunt to find out more but came up empty. Only time would reveal Tom Norris's motive.

Without the colourful Norris, the inquiry might have lost some of its entertainment value. The wait for more startling developments was, however, not long, as a new and unexpected witness was called to the stand in a different location.

What was Tom Norris up to? His surprise withdrawal raised much speculation. Was Ray Munro getting to him? Was he getting out of a case he couldn't win? Was he tired of the limelight? Vancouver was about to find out!

UNSATISFACTORY REASON
Public Confused by Abrupt
Withdrawal of Chief's Lawyer.

Withdrawal of T.G. Norris, Q.C., as Chief Mulligan's counsel in the police probe is completely unsatisfactory to the public.

Citizens are sufficiently puzzled by the progress of the hearings to date without suddenly being told that the lawyer for the key figure has thrown in his hand.

This matter goes far beyond the obligation of a lawyer to his client.

The statement that the reasons for the strange action are entirely "personal to me" fails to recognize the public interest.

Something more than curiosity is involved. Citizens striving to follow the proceedings before this royal commission also have an entirely personal interest in learning whether their lives and personal property were and are being properly protected by the police department.

Mr. Norris as counsel for the police chief set out to convince the commissioner and the public that any suspicion of wrong-doing is groundless. All of a sudden he quits with a statement that he must know is bound to add to the already enormous cloud of rumor and speculation.

With the greatest respect to both Mr. Norris and Royal Commissioner R.H. Tupper, Q.C. , it must be apparent that this cloud will not be dispelled unless some better explanation is adduced. It is to be hoped that the force of this consideration will be impressed upon them and that the public will be taken into their confidence to some greater degree before the books of the hearing are closed.

When Norris quit on September 8, Vancouver Sun *editorial comment showed little sympathy.*

Driving in Police Car

Says She Received King

MULLIGAN'S FRIEND TESTIFIES AT PROBE

The arrival of a heavily disguised mystery lady (right) and her sombre sidekick provided a fresh slant to the Mulligan Affair. John (Jay) Gould, on his first day as Mulligan's new lawyer (see photo below Province *headline), was relegated to second billing by Mulligan's alleged courtesan.*

The Vancouver Province **FINAL**
A Dependable Newspaper

CHIEF GAVE ME GIFTS, GIRL SAYS

Jewels, money

A young woman in a blonde wig and baby-blue hat, who claimed she kept close company with Chief Walter Mulligan for five years at the height of his career, told the Tupper police probe today that the chief gave her $3200 in cash to buy property. She said she believed the money "wasn't from his salary."

*From the
McMorran
Scrapbook*

11.   Femme Fatale

Woman Said Mulligan Gave Her $2,200 for Love Nest.
Province headline

There was an obvious reason for the next break in proceedings. The court house was required for the Fall Assizes, and the probe was forced to move to temporary quarters in city hall, less than a 10-minute drive away. A building with a clock tower located at Cambie and 12th Avenue, city hall was built during the Great Depression of the 1930s. At the time, critics complained it was too far from downtown. Five aldermen also complained about the change of venue, noting that an earlier 1947 police inquiry at city hall had left an "odour." Nevertheless, the seat of local government was, in 1955, the site of the most dramatic and unexpected evidence of the inquiry.

"Woman Said Mulligan Gave Her $2,200 for Love Nest" was the *Province* headline. This added the one ingredient so far missing from this brew of death, bribery, and corruption —sex. On Monday September 12, when the tall woman entered the inquiry room at city hall, Mulligan's expression changed only momentarily as he watched her take the stand. She wore heavy makeup, a wig, glasses, and a floppy-brimmed blue hat and matching coat.

The woman said her name was Helen Elizabeth Douglas and that she was 41. She spoke quietly but firmly and appeared unruffled by the sensation she and her statements were making. She turned away as much as possible from the spectators, directing her attention to Tupper. Reporters dashed from the room to phone in a story on this latest development. Photographers waited outside to get a picture of the "mystery woman."

The inquiry was told that she had recently married and that all counsel had agreed not to mention her new name. As she took the stand a note was passed to Tupper, informing him of his real name, but it was never revealed publicly. Her lawyer, W.W. Lefeaux, asked the press to respect her privacy if it discovered her identity and not to ask questions "for merely sensational news material." Surprisingly, not one reporter used her new name, although the *Sun*'s Wasserman went so far as to give her last initial—"A."

Courtroom artists rendered their own impression of what lay beneath the disguise of Mulligan's friend.

Spectators hung on every word as she described her relationship with Mulligan. Their first meeting was in the Quadra Club in Vancouver, where she was having a quiet birthday celebration. She was his mistress for four years, and she said she saw him about twice a week "both day and night." Tame by today's standards, this was hot, sexy stuff for the media of 1955. Douglas said she went on trips with Mulligan, sometimes in police cars. She attended a chiefs' convention in Montreal and another in Abbotsford, where they met Jack Whelan. On his overnight visits to her Vancouver home, Mulligan often parked well down the street, although it didn't escape the eyes of a neighbour who testified later.

Helen Douglas said Mulligan gave her $2,200 to buy property near Langley, in the Fraser Valley. It was immediately dubbed the "love-nest" by the media. She said he gave the money to her in cash. He also gave her jewellery, later appraised at $500.

Her most sensational statements to Assistant Crown Counsel Vic Dryer concerned Mulligan's admissions over the years concerning illegal activities and payouts to the police. She could not remember many specific names but recalled gamblers Snider and Bancroft. She also heard Mulligan speak of Horton, Ambrose, Plummer, Orr, and Sargent. Douglas said she felt Mulligan was spending more than he made. "I have the impression it didn't come from his salary," she added of the love-nest money.

Mulligan's second lawyer, Jay Gould, who had replaced Norris only days before, was doing a slow but silent burn during her testimony. Finally he exploded in a clash with Dryer. He objected strongly to the hearsay evidence, charging that the proceedings were "impossible" and that rules of evidence were being ignored to produce "evidential confusion."

Douglas said that, although the affair was long over, Mulligan had phoned her three times in the last two months to ask if anyone had contacted her. She told him she had destroyed her diary and got rid of a photograph after the stories broke in *Flash*. Douglas denied knowing or having been approached by Munro, but she had attended a meeting with Prosecutor Stewart McMorran and RCMP inspector Dube, the person Bonner appointed to probe possible criminal aspects arising from testimony.

Asked by Dryer if testifying was the most embarrassing moment of her life, Douglas didn't immediately answer, bit her lip, and finally, almost in a whisper, responded: "Yes." She lost her composure and began to sob gently but then braced herself and held her emotions in check.

Spectators were treated to the evidence of Bill Mitchell, one of Douglas's neighbours in the 3100-block East Georgia. He often saw Mulligan make his visits, arriving in a police car and sometimes parking well down the block. He sometimes witnessed an affectionate farewell in the morning, Douglas in a nightie standing in the doorway kissing the chief.

When Douglas left the inquiry room after her first appearance she was escorted to Mayor Fred Hume's office, where she changed clothes. When she reappeared she hurried through the crowd of reporters and photographers, shielding her face, appropriately enough, with a newspaper. Her lawyer's wife, Mrs. Lefeaux, told reporters (with obvious satisfaction) that Douglas would be disguised as much as possible for her next appearance. "She will be wearing another wig, a school girl hairdo or maybe a red-dyed wig. If necessary we will have plenty of changes of clothes. The photographers will not recognize her," added Douglas's temporary wardrobe mistress. "Every bit of resourcefulness the two of us have will be used to protect her from the public," she said.

Only eight days after his sudden departure Tom Norris was back with a vengeance, lashing out at Ray Munro. On the offensive he painted his ex-client's accuser as the bad guy. Then, with his personal reputation reinforced he again left the inquiry, Mulligan, and Munro behind.

From the McMorran Scrapbook

Much to the pleasure of some, Norris was given the opportunity to grill Ray Munro in more ways than one before he exited the inquiry.

12. Norris Battles Back

*It must not be forgotten that Munro intimidated Cuthbert
and that Cuthbert then shot himself; that Munro intimidated
Superintendent Whelan and Whelan then shot himself.*

Tom Norris

Before Douglas's next quick-change performance, there were new fireworks. The *Sun*'s headline for September 16 read: "Blackmail Made Me Quit Probe."

Tom Norris shattered the morning calm of the probe with an appearance on his own behalf. In a booming voice he charged that Ray Munro had tried to blackmail him. He wanted the reporter brought before Tupper "so that [he could] expose him for what he is." In full oratorical flight, an enraged Norris claimed that Munro and Fleishman between them had intimidated police officers (who later shot themselves) and were now trying to blackmail *him*. His charges sent reporters flying once again, and spectators broke into excited conversations. Tupper, at most times unruffled, looked serious and concerned. He ordered both the accused to appear before the inquiry that afternoon, stressing that this was more important than any other legal business Fleishman might have. They were to attend "without fail."

Norris's anger resulted from a threat by Munro to reveal, in *Flash*, details of a nervous breakdown suffered by the lawyer's daughter. Norris had gone to Tupper after an article threatening to tell the whole story appeared in *Flash* on September 3. He asked for an adjournment, which the commissioner said he could not grant. Later Tupper said that refusal was one of the "hardest decisions I have had to make during these proceedings." It was then that Norris quit as Mulligan's lawyer.

Once again holding *Flash* as though it was contaminated, Norris read an article entitled "Vancouver Merry Go Round," by Ray Munro. There was bitter anger in Norris's voice. This anger was not staged; it was real. He read: "There is a bullish lawyer with a large mouth who's been talking too much under the influence of spirits in front of the members of his exclusive club about people's private lives. This man has no room to talk about other people's personal problems because a member of his family was figured mentally unsound in the recent past. For every nail this alleged 'gentleman' drives into the coffins of other people this reporter will drive one in his through the medium of this column, with no names spared."

Norris revealed he had quit the case in order to fly to Eastern Canada to talk to his daughter. Norris said she had graduated in medicine in 1948 but had suffered a nervous breakdown and had required treatment for a year. He told the inquiry that her illness had placed a great emotional burden on himself, his wife, and his sons. After "years of heartbreak" she had re-established herself in her profession and was interning at a hospital in the East. Norris was told she was doing well and that this revelation would do her no harm. Her reaction, when she heard of the threat, was an immediate and definite, "Go for it."

"I take the greatest pride in her response," stated Norris, adding, "It must not be forgotten that Munro intimidated Cuthbert and that Cuthbert then shot himself; that Munro intimidated Superintendent Whelan and Whelan then shot himself." A Toronto paper tracked down Norris's daughter but did not name either her or the hospital where she worked. The Vancouver media handled it the same way.

When Munro appeared that afternoon in response to Tupper's order, the barely contained fury of Norris was still evident. Despite being named as the writer of the *Flash* column, Munro refused to admit his authorship on the stand. Five times an increasingly angered Norris barked out the question. Munro adamantly refused to respond, stating he would not do so because it might incriminate him. Norris called him a "cowardly cur" and threw down the papers he was holding. Munro was pale but would not answer.

Tupper said he could not force Munro to answer. It also became clear that, in earlier evidence, it had not been clearly established or admitted that Munro had written the articles, although it was obvious that he had. Angered and frustrated almost to the point of tears, Norris, red-faced and in a trembling voice, shouted: "A man who will write that sort of thing and then claim privilege is, I repeat, a cur and a coward!" In support of his client, Fleishman responded that the inquiry had to abide by the law of the land.

While the public was eating up these new revelations and looking forward to the cross-examination of the "mystery woman," the *Sun* printed a front-page editorial criticizing the growing length of the "dragged out probe." The newspaper maintained that Tupper's tea party seemed to be getting out of hand. The editorial said that the inquiry had met on only half of the days available to it since it opened, although it was later explained that much of the time was taken up by RCMP investigations. The *Sun* also complained of the "bewildering hodgepodge of hearsay evidence" and called on Tupper to get down to the "meat of the matter." The *Sun* questioned the work of the prosecuting team, the rising costs to the public, and said that lawyers' bills "could pauperize individuals who may yet be exonerated."

Tupper defended his staff and the time the inquiry was taking, stating publicly that the RCMP probe of some aspects of the case was slowing things down. Investigators were looking into claims of payoffs by Cuthbert to some members of the police gambling squad. Stating that he was neither thin-skinned nor concerned about the criticism, Tupper said the probe would proceed with all speed, but that this might entail being in "second gear or even the lower one."

Among the 40 police volunteers organized by the union to give evidence were eight members of the gambling squad who had worked under Cuthbert. On the stand they were reminiscent of the three monkeys who saw no evil, heard no evil, and spoke no evil. Some even seemed to have little knowledge of their on-the-job responsibilities or the whereabouts of bookies in the downtown area.

Detective John Grimson said he never received graft and never heard of it being paid. He said Cuthbert seemed eager for convictions and never instructed the squad to lay off anybody.

Tupper: "If I was a bookie and was raided, the first thing I would do would be to try and buy you off. But you never heard of it among your associates?"

Grimson: "Only as a joke."

Tupper: "I am surprised at the purity of the underworld."

Detective William Dumaresque gave similar evidence but admitted he had heard a rumour about graft and had a vague memory of something in 1949.

Dumaresque: "It just seems that things were not quite right, that's all."

Tupper "The underworld was apparently incorruptible in that respect."

September ran out with Tupper ruling that contempt charges could not be laid against Munro as Norris had demanded because there was no evidence that he authored the six *Flash* articles named by the lawyer. Commission counsel Hutcheson agreed there was no solid evidence to this effect. Tupper noted that "common sense may show they were written by an individual but that has no validity in law." With common sense shelved in the interests of the law, the public clamoured for more of the mystery lady.

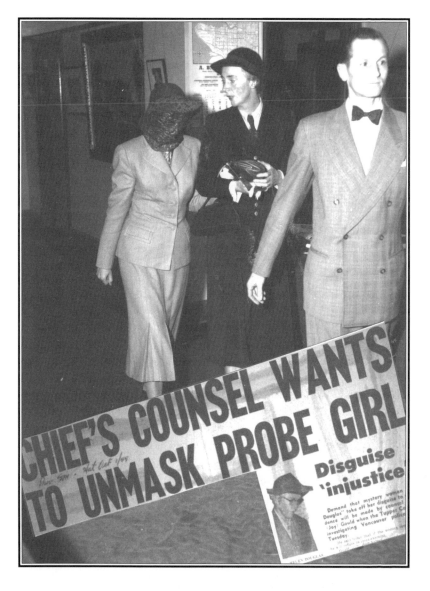

As a court officer led the way for her return engagement the mystery lady again entered court on the supportive arm of Mrs. W.W. Lefeaux. Coming and going the dark veil shielded her from the curious. Jay Gould wanted her unmasked for all.

13.   The Veiled Lady's Ordeal

I have nothing against Mulligan. I am here to tell the truth.
                                            Helen Douglas

Even before the former mistress resumed the witness stand for cross-examination, the public was told it could expect exciting new revelations. Gould told the papers that he would challenge Douglas's appearance in court and demand that her identity not be shielded. He said she had testified "under a false name, wearing a false face and false hair." Gould contended it had been centuries since witnesses had been allowed to testify wearing masks. He argued it was a basic principle of justice that a witness "stand up and be identified for the purpose of cross-examination." He and other counsel had agreed that her new married name not be used—she had been married for two years—but that was before she appeared on the stand partially disguised.

When the hearing resumed Commissioner Tupper unleashed one of his rare flashes of anger. He reprimanded Gould for making statements to the press. Tupper resented the fact that Gould protested the protection of Douglas's identity before arguing his case at the inquiry. Gould followed a now well-worn path, saying the media had gone too far in its story, which "far exceeded" his expectations. This was, of course, baloney. He wanted his views well known, and they were.

About two minutes after her name was called Douglas entered the court wearing a hat with a heavy veil. She lifted the veil and sat facing Tupper but turned round when asked by Gould to do so. He wanted certain people to see her—people obviously brought in by the defence in the hope that they might recognize her from other times and other events. Gould wanted to attack her character and attempt to discredit her evidence. When the veil was lifted a woman in the public benches whipped out a pair of binoculars in order to get a closer look.

Tupper said he did not believe that the witness's appearance in court constituted a disguise. In addition to the brown veil, Douglas wore a brown hat and a light-blue suit. She maintained she had worn heavy glasses for 20 years. Tupper commented that she could wear whatever she wanted outside the room. Gould objected to Mrs. Lefeaux being allowed to sit near the box, but Tupper let her stay.

Gould pressed Douglas on her first meeting with Mulligan in the Quadra Club, but there was nothing to indicate that she was a bar fly or a regular at the club. The witness said she was adopted and that her maiden name was Marjorie Irene Williams. She said she lived at her house on East Georgia and was financially independent because her stepmother had left her an inheritance of exactly $16,690.30—not a fortune but a significant income booster in the late 1940s. Douglas testified that she also had income from two houses in the East End that she owned and rented.

While Douglas described Mulligan as a big spender, her testimony didn't bear this out. She admitted he gave her sums of money, but when asked if they were in the hundreds of dollars she replied they were more in the tens of dollars.

She denied living common law with a man before meeting Mulligan. Gould pressed about evidence from neighbours that she had lots of male visitors. He asked about a sailor, a Captain Wanson of Mobile, Alabama, but Douglas replied he was not an overnight visitor. Gould then worked his way through the other services. He asked about a Royal Canadian Air Force sergeant named Harry, a frequent visitor. "Did he stay all night?" Gould asked. The people in the public gallery leaned forward to hear her answer, their heads swivelling from lawyer to witness like those of spectators at a tennis match. "I was a single woman," Douglas replied. Gould then asked the same question about a French-Canadian army sergeant named Randy. Douglas said he may have. When Gould asked about others, Douglas responded: "I only want to say he who is without sin let him cast the first stone." Spectators seemed to agree.

Gould said Douglas didn't want her picture to appear in the papers because she would be recognized and more would be learned about her. The witness denied this, saying she simply didn't want her picture in the paper because she wanted to try to hold on to some privacy.

She remained unshaken in her contention that Mulligan spent money that "came from gambling . . . not personal gambling but money given to him by gamblers." Gould maintained that Mulligan was merely an easy talker who discussed with her the "cloak-and-dagger" goings-on at the police station. Douglas stuck to her testimony. Spectators chuckled when she said that Mulligan had given her a typewriter on which she used to type the speeches that he made to church groups and various associations and clubs in town.

Douglas maintained that she believed, during their relationship, that Mulligan intended to divorce his wife and marry her. Why their affair ended was not explained. The woman denied a charge by Gould that she was out for revenge and had earlier threatened to tell Mulligan's wife: "I have nothing against Mulligan. I am here to tell the truth." She held up during her ordeal in the box. Gould gave no quarter, but finally the cross-examination was over. Douglas took a half-minute to put on her veil before leaving the room to collapse crying into the arms of Mrs. Lefeaux, while cameramen, reporters, and the public pushed and shoved to get closer.

Helen Douglas had been a convincing witness, with her surprise revelations about Walter Mulligan's secret life. Webster's radio listeners and newspaper readers had little doubt that her confessions were true, and they badly damaged Mulligans credibility. But there was more to come.

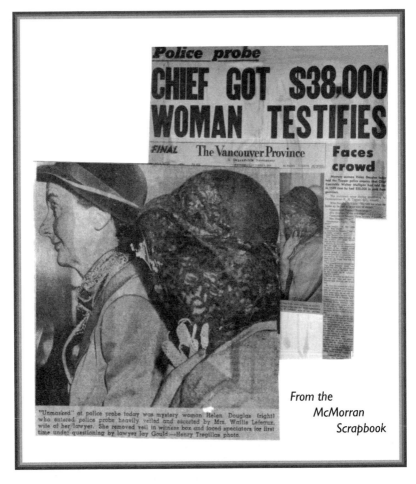

Disguised or not, Helen Douglas proved to be a very credible witness.

*From the
McMorran
Scrapbook*

*Former mayor Charles Thompson (left) sits with investigator T.G. Parsloe
and lawyer Leon Ladner one month into the inquiry. The Vancouver Herald
headline above raised the wrath of commissioner Tupper who deemed its
implications excessive.*

14. Commissioners and Politicians

*If we dismissed him we would have to show cause and we
just couldn't do anything, so we just filed it.*
                                        Mayor Charles Thompson

The various versions of events given by police commissioners and local
politicians left the public baffled. Their statements were rife with confusion,
contradiction, indecision, and timidity. For the most part they had successful
private lives and were highly regarded as citizens of integrity and propriety.
In dealing with Mulligan, however, their decisions and conclusions appeared,
at best, awful. The commissioners probably knew in their hearts that Mulligan
was corrupt, but they liked him. His personal charisma overcame their
suspicions. The secret investigation they had authorized had been a farce,
producing a report that was shoddy and inaccurate. They left Mulligan at the
head of a force that was rife with dissension, wracked by new crisis, and
functioning badly at a time when it was desperately needed to combat rising
crime and the violence of drug wars.

Former mayor Charles Thompson was the first to testify, and he best
exemplified this hapless group. He was a successful car dealer who was
elected mayor in 1948 and turfed out two years later—a one-term wonder.
Automatically chairman of the Police Commission, his feelings and
competence were summed up when he plaintively pondered: "Why the lord
should have allowed this to happen during my term, I don't know."

Thompson met with fellow commissioners after Prosecutor Scott reported
on his 1949 meetings with Leatherdale and Cuthbert. Thompson contacted
Attorney General Wismer about an investigation, but the latter sidestepped
the issue. He claimed he had no manpower, and he felt it was a bad idea to
have the provincial police dig into the Vancouver force. (British Columbia
had its own provincial police force until 1950, when the RCMP took over.)
Wismer also told Thompson that his contact in the provincial force indicated
that there was no corruption in the Vancouver department. He suggested

CHIEF'S LAWYER FAILS TO SHAKE LEATHERDALE

'Views not changed'

Bob Leatherdale proved as unshakable on recall as he was during his first testimony to the inquiry.

using the Pinkerton National Detective Agency from Seattle. This unusual idea was rejected by the commissioners, so Wismer agreed to set up a meeting in Ottawa with the RCMP. Commissioner Rey Sargent flew to the nation's capital but was turned down by the Mounties, who said they would be swamped with other requests if they took on this case. Thompson talked to politicians when he went east for a convention but again got nowhere. This was in sharp contrast to the swift RCMP response in 1955 to two requests from Robert Bonner.

Wismer finally suggested to the three commissioners that they take a quiet look into the matter themselves. He went so far as to provide them with the name of a retired Mountie working in private security who could handle the investigation. T.G. Parsloe, the Tupper Inquiry was told, was hired early in 1950 and turned in a report in June. The ex-Mountie said he used stool pigeons and gamblers he had known, including people he described as agents. One of them got $15 for a day's tailing. Parsloe reported to the Police Commission that "the police department heads are clean and can be trusted implicitly." He also stated that there was "not the slightest semblance of truth" to assertions that Mulligan was engaged in liaisons with the underworld or that he got any money from graft. The ex-Mountie was paid $1,700, including $500 from Mayor Thompson's personal city account.

When called to the stand at the Tupper Inquiry, Parsloe was a terrible witness, strangely unable to remember details of the job and highly embarrassed because his investigation had been such a disaster. He could not or would not name either his informants or the "agents" he had used. Munro's lawyer (Neil Fleishman) challenged Parsloe's veracity and suggested he might not have written the report himself. This was strongly denied. Parsloe's lawyer, Leon Ladner, QC, charged that Tupper's lawyers, Hutcheson and Dryer, were harassing witnesses.

Charles Thompson was ill at ease when cross-examined by Fleishman, who dismissed the report as a "bucket of whitewash." He told Thompson: "As far as you know Parsloe could have written the whole thing at home." The former mayor replied: "That may be true, but I went to the Attorney-General for advice and he recommended the man . . . a former RCMP officer I felt should be capable of doing the job." Thompson added he had not liked the way his predecessors had chosen Mulligan as chief but had developed a "great respect for the man." Asked why no action had been taken, at least against Cuthbert, Thompson replied: "If we dismissed him we would have to show cause and we just couldn't do anything, so we just filed it." He said he would have agreed if Wismer had suggested a public inquiry.

Commissioner Oscar Orr testified he had been uneasy for five years about the situation—an understatement, considering what he knew. There were several significant disclosures in his evidence. Mulligan knew the commissioners had a poor opinion of Cuthbert. Orr revealed that Mulligan had announced Cuthbert's promotion to detective sergeant in police orders before the commissioners had ruled on it and that this was not normal practice. Despite their misgivings, they let the promotion stand.

Orr also disclosed that the *Sun* had early inside information on the Mulligan Affair through its late editorial director, Roy Brown. The commission regarded Brown with great respect and had sought his advice about the graft allegations. Orr stated the commissioners followed Brown's advice "to keep [their] eyes open" and to see what would occur in the future. It was hardly profound advice.

Orr told the inquiry: "We didn't know what to do with Cuthbert, except put him in a safe place, as we thought, somewhere he could do no harm." Orr wasn't sure if the move from gambling to a desk job was at the direction of the chief or the Commission. "I think the chief did it," he reflected. While personally reasonably satisfied with Parsloe's report, Orr admitted we "did nothing but hope for the best."

"We are not running a kindergarten," Orr told the inquiry, although his remarks under cross-examination indicated a lot of hooky was being played. He recalled an occasion when the South Granville area was without police protection because all the squad cars were parked outside the Kerrisdale community hall and all the cops were inside playing poker.

Commissioner Orr said he had taken it upon himself to oppose the union when he felt it was trying to take over the running of the department. He also stated that City Prosecutor McMorran had been working behind the scenes on investigations into the Mulligan Affair before the story appeared in *Flash*. McMorran had talked to potential witnesses, including Munro's informant, ex-cop Jack Whelan. This occurred before McMorran returned to his normal duties that fall as city prosecutor.

GORDON WISMER
...defended former chief

In spite of his legendary noctural profile amid Vancouver's speakeasies, Gordon Wismer seemed to finesse his way through the inquiry, his name or photo rarely attached to any headlines. His relationship with Mulligan was never explored.

When Commissioner Rey Sargent took the stand he described his unproductive trip to Ottawa to try to get RCMP help. He said when Cuthbert confessed to them in 1949 the police department was just settling down after the troubles of 1947—the troubles that brought Mulligan in as chief. He maintained that Cuthbert's statement was inadmissible without corroboration and that the commission was faced with either disrupting the police force again or waiting to see if more evidence turned up. Sargent added that Wismer had given him wait-and-see advice and that he had taken it. A commissioner since 1944, Sargent approved Mulligan's appointment as chief and admitted to the inquiry that "we may have made a mistake by moving him up the ladder too fast." Sargent pointed out that Mulligan had been a friend and favourite of then mayor Gerry McGeer, the commission chairman.

When the probe was announced, Judge Gordon Scott declared he was going to a conference in Britain and that nothing was going to stop his trip. The former city prosecutor was appointed a magistrate in 1953 and was a key figure in the probe but didn't return to Vancouver until September. On the stand he described the police department as a great sieve and rumour mill. "For amusement we would put a rumour on the street to see how fast it would come back," Scott testified.

Scott labelled as "just a passing remark" a statement made to him in a station hallway by Detective George Kitson about Cuthbert's activities. He said it was nothing new, he had already heard it from other sources. Scott recounted that Cuthbert told him at their first meeting in 1949 that Mulligan had "bought" Wismer. The former prosecutor testified he had disagreed with Detective Sergeant Archie Plummer during a 1951 meeting, when Plummer sought a further investigation into the allegations about Mulligan and the bookies. Scott told the probe that "it would be very awkward for [him] to call detectives to get evidence against their own chief." The former prosecutor was quick to allege that the Police Commission was responsible for the handling of the whole affair. He felt that a charge could have been laid against Cuthbert following his 1949 confession, but he left that decision to the commission. Scott confirmed that a major part of Parsloe's report was hopelessly inaccurate in its assessment of the bookie hierarchy.

SCOTT LEFT CUTHBERT ACTION TO COMMISSION

Quizzed at probe

One of Gordon Scott's less compelling reasons for not pursuing Mulligan after Cuthbert's 1949 confessions was, "It's not my job."

In 1951 Fred Hume succeeded Thompson as mayor and head of the Police Commission. He was in office during two of the early reports on graft and corruption, and he knew of the mounting suspicions about Mulligan. He supported the chief, however, right up to the time of the *Flash* revelations. A few weeks prior to Ray Munro's exposé, the commission had received a letter from Mulligan that maintained there was a conspiracy against him —a conspiracy fomented by the media and some politicians. The chief demanded and got a vote of confidence from the commission, an achievement that must have required all of his considerable persuasive talents.

Possibly sparked by these continuing problems and far from everyday decisions, early in 1955 Mayor Hume called on Vancouverites to recognize a Pray Day and to seek divine support and guidance. What Fred prayed for personally makes for interesting speculation.

Wismer had declared from the outset that he would be happy to testify at the inquiry and that he was "as clean as a whistle." The public looked forward to his appearance, but when the former, often flamboyant, attorney general took the stand he, like so many others, could not remember important events. He told the commission: "I have searched my memory. I am not questioning what they say, but it doesn't ring a bell. There were lots of rumours at the time and I remember them asking me what I thought of Mulligan. I told them he was a good policeman." Wismer denied having any "certain arrangements" with Mulligan. He said that the Police Commission and not the attorney general was in control of the department and that he didn't pay any attention to rumours. His insistence that he could not remember the Parsloe Report or much else surprised many, both inside and outside the inquiry. Wismer could not remember being told of Leatherdale's and Cuthbert's statements, although it was he who had assisted in making arrangements for meetings in Ottawa with the RCMP. It was also Wismer who suggested Parsloe do the "secret" investigation. The former attorney general said he didn't know Parsloe but that his name was given to him by a Liquor Board employee and he merely passed it on. Wismer said the first time he met Parsloe was on Hastings Street, when a man came up to him and said, "I'm Parsloe." Gordon Wismer's evidence did nothing to inspire confidence in either the commissioners or the politicians on the perimeter of Mulligan's world.

Because the Mulligan Affair centred around a public inquiry rather than a court of law, many of the lawyers involved advised their clients to admit as little as possible. And once one major player got away with the loss-of-memory ploy, it became the standard course for a host of others.

15.   Mulligan Makes His Move

[The original Mounties' probe was] *the brainchild of an over-enthusiastic young prosecutor and a man who works in the cesspool of journalism.*

Jay Gould

Tupper Inquiry aficionados—those who showed up to pack the public benches, those who read every word the *Sun*, *Province*, and *Herald* printed, and those who hung on reporter Webster's nightly utterances—were gearing up for the appearance of Walter Mulligan. From the outset they had looked forward to this high point of the case, but October 12 did not produce the climax they all expected.

Mulligan's lawyer Jay Gould had become increasingly angry during the examination of the chief's former mistress and had seethed throughout the ensuing month. He complained frequently that hearsay evidence was introduced and that it was extremely damaging to his client. He attacked Tupper for the handling of the situation and for allowing rumours to be repeated. He claimed that Tupper had acted as both prosecutor and inquisitor. Tupper, unphased by Gould's comments, repeated that it was his duty to "inquire and report." Observers wondered how far Gould would go, but Tupper remained placid. He said he was considering a further adjournment in order to receive more information from the RCMP's continuing investigations. It was apropos that Tupper dug into his classical learning to introduce the name of Tomas de Torquemada, a medieval inquisitor. Tupper suggested that he and de Torquemada shared similar mandates, and he said it would be as useless for counsel to take exception to his handling of the case as it would have been for them to take exception to de Torquemada's handling of the Inquisition. Tupper pointed out that it was only natural justice and the criminal code that "prevent[ed] [him from] sending someone to the torture." It was assumed that the commissioner, never a load of laughs, was joking.

The thought of thumb screws didn't bother the angry Gould, who accused Tupper of using all the authority of a Supreme Court judge without accepting the responsibility. "You have carte blanche right to carry out a 20th century inquisition here." Tupper restated that the inquiry differed from a criminal case. Gould complained that Mulligan had already been destroyed by gossip and hearsay, adding that his client was prepared to stand trial "where there are rules of cross-examination." Gould strongly protested any new adjournment, which he said would leave Mulligan "dripping with the mud of rumour for months."

When Tupper ignored this plea Gould played his final card. He blasted the Mounties' original probe as "the brainchild of an over-enthusiastic young prosecutor and a man who works in the cesspool of journalism." (He was, of course, referring to McMorran and Munro, respectively.) He said the prosecution had a "lugubrious hope they might stumble on something." Then voicing total disagreement with Tupper's interpretation of his role, Gould stunned all present by stating that he and Mulligan were withdrawing from the inquiry. The urbane Tupper announced an immediate adjournment but not before he expressed hope that Mulligan would continue to have legal counsel. Gould replied he would inform the chief of his rights, and the lawyer and his client walked away smiling as the inquiry adjourned *sine die* (i.e., with no date fixed for a further meeting).

In a statement to the press, Attorney General Bonner backed Tupper's handling of the inquiry, noting that it would be "reprehensible in the extreme" for him to interfere with the proceedings and repeating that Tupper had latitude not available in a regular trial.

Late in October Mulligan made the move that by now many felt was inevitable. In a letter to the Police Commission he asked to be relieved of his job, noting: "My further usefulness as chief constable has ended." The letter reiterated that hearsay evidence, rumour, and innuendo were responsible for his situation and that he had no more money than any other person who lived modestly on a good salary. He had been on paid leave of absence since the crisis broke in June. Monetarily it would be to his advantage to be fired rather than to resign. Through the inquiry many observers came to feel that Mulligan's $10,236-a-year salary was inadequate for a chief of police in a major city, with some 700 people under his command. If he retired he would get only the amount he had paid into the pension fund, but if he was fired he would be eligible for a slightly larger pension (estimated at about $100 per month).

Mulligan's powers of persuasion did not fail him. Four city aldermen immediately said he should be fired. In a newspaper poll that questioned 200 people, 176 felt he should be fired and given the extra money. A few days later his request was granted. Friends said the realization that he was through made Mulligan "sick at heart." One commented bitterly that the Police Commission, which had always said good things about Mulligan, "couldn't

EXTRA **The Vancouver Province** EXTRA

MULLIGAN ASKS TO BE LET OUT

'For morale of force'

Money conscious until the end, Mulligan asked the Police Commission to discharge him (rather than forcing him to quit) so that he could maximize his pension.

find a good word at the end." The press reported that Mulligan and his wife had left town temporarily to get out of the spotlight, but that report later proved to be inaccurate.

Mayor Hume said a new police chief might be hired on a temporary basis, for six months to two years, pending receipt of Tupper's full report. Then a permanent chief would be hired, although he admitted they might have to increase the salary to get the right man. The *Sun* urged the mayor not to hire anyone until all the facts were in, pointing out that the department had worked seemingly efficiently for four months without a chief. "A new chief hired now who was a paragon of virtue and ability still would not make any difference until all the facts are in," added the paper.

Tupper announced he was going to Victoria to talk to the RCMP about its investigations and to give a progress report to Bonner. Responding to press queries he noted that there had been no criticism from the attorney general about the handling of the inquiry.

The fourth estate was less tolerant. The *Sun* joined the fray with another blistering editorial that was highly critical of the inquiry commission. Once more it called on Attorney General Bonner to speed up proceedings. The papers also backed Gould's complaints about hearsay evidence. They took particular exception to Douglas being allowed to testify without using her present name and to the fact that nothing had been done following Munro's refusal to say he had written the articles in *Flash*. The *Sun* noted that Tupper had stated his intention to get the probe over quickly, but it had now lasted

The deal to get rid of the police chief was rubber-stamped in under an hour, and Mulligan, after 8½ years as top cop, became just another ex-cop on an early pension. After their meeting Commissioners Rey Sargent (centre) with Mayor Hume and Oscar Orr (right) all repeated "the opinion of this board is that the usefulness of Walter H. Mulligan as chief constable of the city of Vancouver is now at an end."

four months, with no end in sight. However, Bonner's words to the press were: "I cannot intervene no matter what I might feel."

In early November Magistrate Oscar Orr resigned from the Police Commission, maintaining that his move had nothing to do with the probe, although few believed him. Orr, who had been appointed in 1948, added to their suspicions when he commented: "I can tell you anyone would be glad to get out of that." Wounded at Ypres in the First World War, and Chief Prosecutor for Canada at the Japanese war crimes trials in the Second World War, Orr said he was going to India to visit the grave of his son, who was killed in the last World War. It was his opinion that the probe would wind up in three to four months. Although Mayor Hume supported former prosecutor Gordon Scott for the job, the provincial government immediately appointed 50-year-old Vancouver lawyer and war hero Brigadier William Murphy, CBE, DSO, to replace Orr.

As the rains of November doused Vancouver, Neil Fleishman announced that he had had enough of Ray Munro and was quitting as his lawyer. He sent a short, terse note to his client: "The writer of this letter no longer wishes to be in receipt of your instructions. Will you kindly retain other counsel at your earliest convenience." Munro said he would not hire another lawyer, announcing with bravado and in his usual style: "I will stand alone."

Vancouver's obsession with the probe was flagging, and the public had something else to concentrate on as November ran out. The city was agog about hosting its first Grey Cup, just having been admitted to the Canadian Football League. The battered league of today would die for a smidgeon of the enthusiasm that swept the city as the Edmonton Eskimos and Montreal Alouettes battled for the cup. Alberta won. Fans packed the downtown area for a huge parade, street dancing, and parties.

Tupper had recessed the probe, but the police continued to make ham-fisted news. The publicity, suspicion, revelations, and innuendo from the hearing were getting to them. When a reporter went to Superintendent Jack Horton for some straightforward news, he was told: "It's none of the public's business." The reporter had been asking about police arrangements for the Grey Cup. Horton added: "It's been none of the public's business for a number of years and it's getting less and less its business every day. If any elected official wants to know what is going on he can come down. No newspaper is going to play city hall." Acting Chief Rossiter rushed in with some damage control, saying the paper had a "bit of substance" to its complaint about police censorship and that he would talk to the commission about it.

Relations between the police and the media continued to deteriorate. The *Sun* took issue with the fact that 22 of 23 new cars being acquired by the department would go to senior officers for personal use. Wasserman's sharp pen noted that each car would bear the city crest and motto: "By Land and Sea We Prosper."

December began with tragedy for the police department when Constable Gordon Sinclair was gunned down while investigating a break-in. He was the twelfth Vancouver policeman to die in the line of duty, and he was alone on patrol. Mulligan's introduction of one-man cars had always been a bitter point with the police union. Sinclair was a longtime member of the force, popular with his colleagues, and a founder of the police pipe band. Some 400 attended his funeral, feelings heightened by the strain of the last few months of the probe. Joe Gordon, well known to the police, was arrested within days, successfully tried for murder and later hanged at Oakalla.

Before the end of 1955 the public learned that the top candidate for the chief's job was Superintendent George Archer, the man who had assigned two Mounties to assist with the investigation of the department during the Mulligan probe. Archer had been 35 years with the RCMP and was due to retire. It was announced that he would take the job for $12,000 per year, with an $8,000 bonus for "revitalizing" the force. While some quibbled about the money, others thought it was worth any price to clean up the mess. Archer ultimately became the chief. A stiff disciplinarian, he is often credited with being one of the best chiefs in Vancouver police history.

Following Gordon Sinclair's slaying, new police commissioner William Murphy told city council it could have a first-rate force within three years if it would spend enough money and let Vancouverites "get along with a few less rose bushes in Stanley Park." This was a bold statement, the suggestion of depriving the park of some of its roses being regarded by some as near heresy. The brigadier pointed out that Sinclair, like most other city police of his generation, had never had any formal training. Recruits had been pushed into the street for on-the-job experience, and the training budget for the entire department that year was only $500. Murphy said the public perception of a policeman was of "a fat man with a billy stick." He urged scrapping the one-man car system. In light of all that was going on, Murphy was playing a strong hand. A few days later, Acting Chief Rossiter announced the start of a training program and the end of one-man patrol cars. On Friday, December 30, the papers carried pictures of Archer's swearing in. He started work the following Monday morning.

Three hours after taking over, Archer announced changes in the department. Gordon Ambrose had the new title of deputy chief (instead of assistant chief), and Alan Rossiter was named the executive staff superintendent. Archer met 200 members of the force and said he would parade them occasionally. He demanded "shined shoes, pressed uniforms and short hair," but the public was looking for a lot more. The department put its foot in it again, when Ambrose passed a report to the Police Commission stating that young hoodlums must be driven out of the city, put in jail, or made to join the armed forces. The latter fired back immediately, stating loudly and clearly that they wanted no part of any thugs.

After a three-month adjournment, Tupper's probe resumed in mid-January. While media and public interest remained fairly high, Mulligan's withdrawal reduced the chance of any exciting new revelations. Commission Counsel George Hutcheson and Assistant Counsel Vic Dryer told Tupper that they had talked to nearly everyone who might have a bearing on the case. Hutcheson said it would be unjust to produce statements that could not be supported, pointing out that counsel had no case to prove, as it was an inquiry, not a criminal case.

Probably stung by Gould's attack, and influenced by others who wanted to soft-pedal the hearsay evidence, Tupper stepped in when Ray Munro resumed giving evidence. Spectators had perked up because, with Munro on the stand, almost anything was possible. He quickly tossed out allegations and a list of names, ranging from Detective George Kitson to Quadra Club boss William Couper, who had recently disappeared from Vancouver. Tupper told him it would be "most improper" to bring unfounded reports and accusations before the public. He added that they must try to "save the reputations of people." Gould must have had an ironic "I-told-you-so" laugh.

Munro had long since quit *Flash*. The preceding July he had told the inquiry that he was through with the tabloid as of August. He told the papers that he intended to publish his own tabloid, *Tab Weekly*, but, like many of his schemes, the project fell apart. Munro admitted in a radio interview with

ARCHER NAMED AS NEW POLICE CHIEF

The Vancouver Sun — FINAL EDITION

Ottawa Gives Okay

With the RCMP's blessing a no-nonsense mountie with the ability to turn the police force around assumed duties in January.

From the McMorran Scrapbook

Webster that his money was gone and he was broke. The radio man said later that he was amazed at the number of people who called offering Munro financial assistance. Whatever Ray Munro was, he had always captured people's imaginations.

Munro's hatred of Mulligan was unabated and, when asked at the inquiry if he was out to get the chief, he replied without hesitation: "Yes." He added that Mulligan knew all about the lottery racket and also had cases of liquor delivered to him from the Quadra Club. Munro claimed personal knowledge of payoffs: "In a year as a newspaperman I have come to learn a great many things." (While Munro had been a news photographer for a number of years, his stint as a reporter/photographer consisted of about a year on the *Province* plus a few weeks as editor of the western edition of *Flash*.)

In typical Munro fashion, and with the flamboyance he loved, he hauled out a plaque. He told Tupper he didn't know where it came from. He explained that it had been delivered to his apartment. It was written in Munro's kind of language, and he read it to the inquiry without a blush: "Presented to Ray Munro for his courageous efforts as a newspaper reporter for making a policeman's life a happier one. From his friends in the uniform branch of the

Vancouver Police Department, Christmas 1955." At the bottom it read: "There walks a man." There were more than a few who wondered if he had sent it to himself. Questioned later about the plaque Munro stated: "I feel there is a slight stigma attached to it now." He admitted it was possible that some senior or junior officers had made it "in the hope that I might make a fool of myself here."

Munro's plaque was Exhibit No. 102. The shorthand reporter's verbatim notes are part of the transcript held in the provincial archives in Victoria, transferred years ago from the Attorney General's Office. They record that the plaque was "returned to owner." None of the other exhibits was returned quickly to those who presented them, and some lawyers wondered why this exhibit was so speedily returned to Munro. There was no explanation.

Munro appeared intent on taking down anyone remotely related to Mulligan. He raised the name of traffic officer Richard Mullock, who was Mulligan's nephew. He alleged that, while on duty, Mullock had participated in a drinking party at the home of Murray Goldman, a Vancouver haberdasher who at the time had a store adjacent to the *Province* building on West Hastings. Goldman was, in those days, a frequent player in Wasserman's column. Mullock maintained he and another traffic officer went to Goldman's house to investigate reports of illegally parked cars. Mullock said Goldman apologized for being out of liquor and not able to offer them a drink, although they did have a sandwich.

Munro's evidence rambled. Lawyer Nicholas Mussallem, who appeared for Mullock, took Munro to task, reminding him of Norris's "cowardly cur" denouncement. Munro maintained that, through his associating with *Flash*, "[he] lost the reputation [he] previously enjoyed." His obsession with Mulligan was emphasized when he told the inquiry: "Somebody has to bring a stop to this crime wave . . . if anyone can do it, I can do it. I want him out of a job, out of the police department and clean this place up."

Mulligan was already out but Munro couldn't let go, and Mussallem wasn't prepared to let him off easily. The lawyer demanded to know if his discharge from the air force had been for psychological reasons. Munro became agitated and angry, declaring he had had three crashes but was never considered unsound. He was further outraged when questioned about a story he wrote claiming his airplane had been fired on from the ground while flying over Sons of Freedom Doukhobor territory in the Kootenays. Mussallem suggested that police investigators found that the bullet holes had entered the top side of the wing and not the bottom. Munro yelled his angry denial.

When Mussallem pressed on with more personal questions about the reporter and his lifestyle, Munro bitterly told the hearing that "this [was] another attempt to bare the tragedies of the witnesses' life." Munro's statement drew no sympathy from members of the public, some of whom noted that the

When Ray Munro went after Mulligan's nephew, traffic cop Richard Mullock (left) and his partner George Burton, their lawyer turned the tables on him.

dashing reporter could dish it out but couldn't take it. An agitated Munro shouted out that Mulligan had been the head of the whole phoney lottery racket.

The next news to break caught Vancouver by surprise. Mulligan, they learned, had skipped the country back in December after applying for landed immigrant status in the United States. Jay Gould said his client had emigrated before Christmas, as soon as the US counsel's office confirmed his status.

Taking all his possessions with him, Mulligan, no longer a policeman, intended to go into business in Los Angeles. His flight raised questions and criticism, including charges in the BC Legislature that the authorities had been lax in letting him go. Opposition politicians implied that his departure had been aided and abetted by friends in high places who were anxious to see him out of the way. US authorities maintained that when his application was received they had no idea who he was. The point was also made that there were no criminal charges of any kind against Mulligan, for Tupper had not yet released his report. Former police commissioner Oscar Orr, now returned from India, commented that Mulligan's application for a visa was no secret and that many knew of his plan.

16.   The Final Days

*I know him to see him. Yes. He raided my place a lot of
times.*

Joe Celona

While the public was robbed of Mulligan's version of the story, the row about
his flight sparked new interest in the few remaining witnesses. This was the
period when evasive manoeuvres stretched the imagination and when truth
was pushed to the outer limits. Most of those testifying now suffered from
an overwhelming loss of memory. Despite this, they managed to convey
insights into the seamier side of life.

Angelo Branca was the new lawyer on the stand. A firebrand who
defended a lot of criminals in his long career, Branca wound up a much
respected QC and BC Appeal Court judge. He recalled with relish some of
his brushes with the bench when defending clients. Branca had been one of
the leading lights in a star-studded defence lineup during the famous 1952
bookie conspiracy case. Mayor Fred Hume had ordered the investigation,
and all the city's leading bookmakers were charged. Archie Plummer told
the inquiry he felt Mulligan and Cuthbert should have been included among
those prosecuted in 1952. Charges involved conspiracy to create a gambling
ring using common race-result wire services and information sheets. The
trial included all the components of a case from the era of Al Capone. A
leading witness was savagely beaten by two gun-wielding masked men when
he returned to his West Vancouver home. After 22 days of testimony, the
verdict was a major setback for the city prosecutor and the Police Commission.
It was a victory for the defence and, particularly, for Branca when the jury
declared all 26 accused conspirators not guilty after only a few hours of
deliberation. Branca had defended eight of them.

During the Mulligan Affair Angelo Branca defended Bruce Snider, a
previously convicted bookie, who denied any knowledge of protection money
paid to Mulligan. Branca was also lawyer for Joe Celona, who had been a
Vancouver vice-lord since the 1920s, well known to police, mayors, and
criminals of all kinds. He was sentenced to 21 years in jail in 1935 for running

Vancouver's largest prostitution racket. Only five years later, he was quietly released. There was speculation that money and politics played a part in his early release.

Angelo Branca's client, in typical underworld style, staged a noisy confrontation that enlivened waning public interest in the Mulligan Affair. Branca himself was involved in the hallway altercation outside Tupper's chambers. Celona had been identified as the operator of a bookie joint frequented by police. He had seldom been photographed and took a punch at *Vancouver Sun* photographer Brian Kent as soon as the latter's flash went off. It was probably the first time the immortal words "You dirty rat" had been uttered outside an old Hollywood set. Branca made a lunge at Kent's camera, saying he would smash it. The pictures appeared, and Celona and Branca were charged. When Celona next appeared at the inquiry, there were a dozen photographers in the hall determined to get his picture. He turned the tables, however. Instead of leading a mad pursuit through the halls of justice, Celona, smiling and wearing his gangster-style hat, welcomed the cameramen and even posed for pictures.

When the case involving *Sun* photographer Kent eventually came to court, Celona said he was trying to shield his face with his hat and just lashed out blindly. He maintained he had actually called out, "Blackmailing rats." He was fined $25. To no one's surprise, Branca was acquitted.

Evidence was given by police witnesses to the effect that over the years, when checking out Celona's East Hastings establishment, they had been surprised to learn from him of upcoming transfers within the department and other police business. In giving evidence, Celona testified that he was actually just helping the officers who happened upon his place in their hunt for the murderers of Danny Brent (of university golf course fame) and the assailants of "Silent Bill" Semenik.

The public galleries again erupted in laughter when Celona was asked if he knew a certain Detective Grant. He replied: "I know him to see him. Yes. He raided my place a lot of times."

Comic relief was also provided at the inquiry by Nick Badick, a minor underworld figure called to the stand to give evidence about bootlegging. No one appreciated the situation more than Branca: "Your conviction in July, 1945, was for possession of an offensive weapon. What was that offensive weapon?"

Badick: "You ought to know, you defended me."

While most in the room roared with laughter, the unfazed Branca pressed on: "You were convicted of contributing to juvenile delinquency. What were the details?

Badick: "You ought to know. You were my lawyer then."

MULLIGAN OUT OF REACH OF PROBE, NOW IN U.S.

POLICE PROBE VIOLENCE

PRINCIPALS IN ERUPTION OF VIOLENCE AGAINST CAMERAMEN AT PROBE

Celona Attacks Sun Man, Lawyer Damages Camera

Mulligan Moves To Los Angeles

Ex-Chief Out of Reach Of Tupper Police Probe

MULLIGAN REQUES COPY OF REPOR

City's crime rate continent highest

Ex tall Pro

Probe will end Friday

Bancroft on stand

e, Murphy e board of 4

JOE CELONA

GEO. SUTHERLAND named by Tupper

As the hearing wound down, all that was left for entertainment was the various comments from local lowlifes and bookies who took the stand. Joe Celona (behind hat at top of page) and his lawyer, Angelo Branca, were charged in a fracas with cameraman Brian Kent.

To the roar of more laughter, Branca noted with a grin: "Today I am not. You may wish I were!"

Branca also represented Inspector Pete Lamont, whom Celona's former common-law wife said she saw in the gambler's place playing poker. Norma Moore was an unwilling witness, a drug addict who was brought to the hearing from jail, where she was serving six months for vagrancy (which, in those days, usually meant prostitution). She testified she saw several policemen at Celona's, including Donald MacDonald and Jack Horton, and she testified that she saw Celona count out a lot of money in front of Lamont. She added that Celona always knew when a raid was coming "because of police stool pigeons."

Mrs. Rose Corning

Constable Lorne Tompkins then took the stand and testified that he saw a large amount of money passed to Lamont in another suspected bookie joint. Mrs. Rose Corning, widow of the late bookie "Mugs" Corning, said she saw white envelopes containing money going to Lamont and MacDonald. On one occasion she opened one and found $300 in it. Branca told Tupper that, in his two terms as head of the gambling squad, Lamont made more arrests than anybody else. He maintained that Mrs. Corning was mistaken in identifying Lamont as a cop who took money. A feisty character who had done a lot of living, Mrs. Corning said at one time she had talked to Mulligan about lotteries. She told Tupper she had lost twelve pounds recently, worrying about the effects of her testimony on the families of Lamont and MacDonald. Branca produced other witnesses who said that whoever she saw taking the envelopes, it wasn't his client. Branca quizzed her about events that had occurred some ten years earlier, but she didn't miss a beat or fudge an answer, commenting in words that the spectators appreciated: "I will have to leave it up to you, Mr. Commissioner, to decide who is telling the truth. The odds are three to one against me ... it's high even for a bookie's wife." Tupper's final report spoke kindly of Mrs. Corning.

Former detective Percy Alan Hoare told of being offered bribes by gamblers and telling his superiors about it. One of the bookies he spoke of was the intriguing "Milo the Hatter on West Pender." Hoare testified that Milo had offered him $1,000 for protection. He also said a Mrs. Lim from Chinatown had proposed payment of $600 to $700 a month each for some seven gambling houses she owned.

POLICE PROBE TO HEAR NEW PAYOFF EVIDENCE

Joe Celona went from camera-shy local bookie to an accommodating "happy face" once he learned to enjoy the publicity rather than fight it.

Leo Bancroft testified he had been a bookie for 30 years and was never charged. He said he gave it up on doctor's advice but worked with Snider in running racehorses and a dairy.

Quadra manager Gordon Towne testified that Ray Munro had visited the club and attempted to extort $3,000 from him. Barman Joe Smith maintained he overheard Munro make the attempt.

As the inquiry drew to its conclusion, Cuthbert's lawyer engaged in a last-ditch defence of his client. Oliver said his client had been subjected by Norris to the widest, most sweeping and violent cross-examination imaginable. He claimed that in rummaging through every closet in Cuthbert's life, Norris had "failed to come up with a skeleton or even a small bone." Oliver insisted that Cuthbert had been involved with Mulligan for only a short time in his long career and that his client had received many commendations as a policeman. The lawyer also pointed out that Cuthbert had not run away but had stayed to face the music.

There were other minor witnesses, but on January 27, 1956, the hearing came to a close in an almost empty room at 3:07 p.m. The public had had enough. More than 1.2 million words of subjective and sometimes contradictory evidence had been uttered in 40 sitting days spread over seven months beginning in June, 1955. There were 126 witnesses and 144 exhibits. More than 300 people had been interviewed by commission officials and RCMP investigators. One unidentified lawyer was reported to have received a fee of $12,000—a lot of money in the 1950s. There were sweeping indictments against Mulligan and the Vancouver police. The ex-chief had elected not to give his side of the story that became the top Canadian news event of 1955. What did it all mean? Tupper promised to bring down his report as soon as possible.

17.   Mulligan Nailed

*It would not be the first occasion when the tragic
degeneration of a man's character arose from such a liaison
as she recounted.*

Commissioner Reg Tupper

Mulligan was branded a crook in Tupper's 75,000-word report tabled in the
BC Legislature by Attorney General Robert Bonner on February 29. The
newspaper headlines screamed: "Mulligan Got Graft" and "Mulligan Took
Bribes."

Tupper found Mulligan capable but corrupt, a man who had bolted to
the United States because he knew he couldn't clear his name. The
commissioner stated that bookies Wallace and Sutherland paid bribes to
Cuthbert and that these bribes were split with Mulligan. These were the only
people Tupper actually accused of graft and corruption. After sifting through
all the evidence and hearsay presented, however, he indicated there were
others. He said the racket could not have worked without the collusion of
some members of Cuthbert's 12-man gambling squad, despite the fact that
the RCMP investigation under Inspector Dube failed to come up with sufficient
evidence to lay charges against any of them. The Dube Report was a
disappointment to those who assessed its value. As has been said, it was
never made public and today cannot be found. Tupper rejected charges that
hearsay evidence, rumour, and innuendo had crucified the former chief and
said that all his conclusions were based on evidence that would have been
admissible in a court of law. He found no "improper association" between
Mulligan and former attorney general Wismer (the very fact that he addressed
the issue, however, helped many readers conclude that there was). Tupper
also wrote that Mulligan had mistrusted his subordinates and "did not have
the confidence and respect of a large number of those under his command."

In his interim report delivered a month earlier, Tupper was, in view of
the high crime rates, critical of the Police Commission's performance. He

In his final report Tupper juggled the controversial and at times contradictory evidence from many witnesses. He exonerated the senior officers and all other policemen, with the exception of Mulligan and Cuthbert. He left no doubt, however, that there were accomplices, particularly members of the gambling squad. He said investigations failed to come up with conclusive evidence that could be taken to court. He found Cuthbert's main problem to be a "lack of character" but called him "a kindly man who could be easily swayed by others."

warned city council to stop penny-pinching and to provide more money for badly needed policing. He stressed that law and order were neither properly nor efficiently enforced.

Tupper said that any proceedings against Mulligan and Cuthbert would be initiated by the special three-man committee appointed by Bonner to review the inquiry's testimony. The panel consisted of Stewart McMorran, Vic Dryer, and Alex Patterson of the Attorney General's Office. Few observers had doubted Tupper would nail Mulligan and Cuthbert, and many hoped the ex-chief would be formally charged and brought back from the US to face charges. There was a general feeling of disappointment with the lack of action taken after the months of revelations and sensational evidence. Critics said it was a whitewash. One *Province* editorial questioned whether the public expense had been justified by the findings and "the seven months of ponderous, labyrinthine investigations." A *Calgary Herald* observer wrote that it was a "Hollywood-B" production that added no lustre to the reputation of Royal Commissions in Canada—a cry echoed to this day.

Some of Tupper's toughest criticism was directed at Munro, whom he said "[thought] of the world in terms more suitable to a melodrama than to the usual though sometimes tragic circumstances of everyday life." He charged that Munro was "unable to dispense with sensationalism and has found that it arises more easily in exposing the wrongs of others." He pointed to Munro's statement during cross-examination that "the end justifies the means, a pernicious doctrine which has no place in its accomplishment for justice or truth." The commissioner condemned *Flash,* which he described as richly deserving the title of scandal sheet. He noted that even Munro had testified that his reputation had suffered because of his association with the tabloid. It was obvious that Munro got much of his information from Jack Whelan, whom Tupper described, albeit in more judicial terms, as a fantasizing screwball.

In response to the report, Jack Whelan immediately stated that he stood by his story, and Munro took his usual modest bow, saying: "If I had to do it again it would be worthwhile just to clean out the police department."

Tupper proved himself to be a man with a unique and discerning palate for truth. He based his findings largely on the evidence of three people— Helen Douglas, Bob Leatherdale, and Len Cuthbert. He painted Douglas as a *femme fatale* but said that her evidence formed a believable story, if not a complete one. If anyone emerged from the inquiry with credit, it was Leatherdale, and "if there was agreement on one significant fact it [was] that he [was] to be believed." Cuthbert's main problem had been a lack of character, commented Tupper, who added that the policeman was a kindly man easily swayed by others.

The commissioner blamed the ex-mistress for much of Mulligan's downfall. "It would not be the first occasion when the tragic degeneration of a man's character arose from such a liaison as she recounted," wrote Tupper, who, unfailingly polite and courteous, had cast a few straight-laced looks during the evidence given by some of the women who appeared during the long probe.

Douglas had kept company with Mulligan from 1944 to 1949 and had been a reluctant witness, not a seeker of revenge. She appeared only because she had been summoned. "Her appearance here has nothing to do with wanting to get back after five-and-a-half years against the man who spurned her as a prospective wife." Tupper found that her story "explain[ed] in part the corrupt behaviour of a man capable in many ways who impressed the members of the Police Commission with his abilities as well as the public at large."

The commissioner cleared Mulligan in the "piggy bank" caper (as told by Whelan and as it appeared in *Flash*). Tupper obviously had been intrigued by Whelan, with his *Guys-and-Dolls* style and language, his fantasies, his various careers, and his range of cohorts, but he found him inconsistent—to say the least— and an "irresponsible witness."

While there were many lawyers who shared Gould's views about hearsay evidence and Tupper's overall handling of the probe, the commissioner maintained he had properly managed his task of ferreting out information

Photographed from the back pages of the McMorran scrapbook, one final news clipping sums up R.H. Tupper's final report. Mulligan "accepted bribes." Cuthbert was "of weak moral fibre." Ray Munro "lives in a world of melodrama, feeds on sensationalism." Helen Douglas was "believable."

from within a mass of contradictory evidence and claims, and he made no excuses for it: "All conclusions reached upon the conduct of any persons are founded on the evidence . . . which would have been admissable in a court of law."

The lawyers and the press had criticized the inquiry's many adjournments. Tupper pointed out that most were taken up with continuing RCMP investigations into the actions of the gambling squad and that the longest was three months at the end of 1955. Much public criticism centred on this aspect of the inquiry—a criticism based upon a "no-smoke-without-fire" belief. There was Leatherdale's view that a large number of the squad were on the take and Cuthbert's refusal to clear more than four of its 12 members. There was also the sweeping memory loss on the stand, which drew critical comment from Tupper. He declared that the position of the other eight squad members was "an unhappy one which must trouble any person called upon to express an opinion on their conduct." There was sufficient evidence to point to the possibility "that some of these men were implicated in some of the payoffs Cuthbert received." There was no corroboration of Cuthbert's claim, and the commissioner found that "there [was] no firm and sufficient grounds for the allegation that any of these men [had] been corrupt."

Referring to testimony to the effect that Joe Celona knew of changes in the detective branch before any announcements were made, Tupper found that, "either by negligence or [the] improper design of some police officer," the gambler had inside information he should not have possessed. Tupper added that, at this time, "Celona may have been involved in part in the conspiracy which in my opinion existed between Mulligan and Cuthbert."

In a compelling indictment against Mulligan and Cuthbert, Tupper wrote: "It is my opinion that two police officers have engaged in corrupt practices; one, and the junior of them, stood to face and admit the allegations against him; the other did not." He described the whole story as a "tragic narrative of personal temptation and wrong-doing." Tupper found that Cuthbert was a competent police officer but "a man with a grave weakness of character."

Tupper "regretted" that Mulligan had not testified, a feeling shared by the public and the press, who had been anticipating a fighting comeback from the usually combative ex-chief. He carefully noted, however, that "only the simple, uninformed, or the malign could suggest Mulligan would give answers which might tend to incriminate himself."

There was severe censure of the conduct of former Vancouver alderman and former MLA Jack Price. Tupper found it "as disconcerting as anything that came before the inquiry." The commissioner was troubled that, when Jack Whelan went to Price and asked him for help to get immunity from alleged interference with his club operation, Price didn't go to the Police Commission. Instead, he went to Couper of the Quadra Club and bookmaker Snider. Tupper stated that Price "tacitly accepted" a situation that permitted a club secretary and a gambler to determine how Vancouver's police force should be disposed. Tupper's focus on this event possibly says more about him than it does about Price. Price, in essence, was singled out for ignoring a system that Tupper concluded was not working.

Tupper surprised many with the speed of both his interim and his final reports, although obviously much had been written during the last long adjournment. His interim report had arrived on Bonner's desk in January. The 50,000-word document dealt with law enforcement in general and the administration of the Vancouver Police Department in particular.

The commissioner was critical of everything from city funding of the police force to the performance of the Police Commission and its disastrous stewardship. Being particularly critical of former mayor Thompson, Tupper noted that Cuthbert should have been fired following his 1949 revelations and that Mulligan should have been confronted immediately. He blasted the secret Parsloe Report as useless and inept. "My inquiry has brought me to the firm conclusion that the Criminal Code of Canada is neither properly nor efficiently enforced by the City of Vancouver. There is laxity in enforcement and such laxity has been present for many years." Tupper went on to note that a six-month training course for recruits was a burning necessity and that a fourth member of the Police Commission was needed to help balance the workload.

A number of administrative issues emerged from the inquiry. Tupper found no evidence of favouritism in Mulligan's system of promotions and was not opposed to his methods. He said that the city charter must be changed to permit the chief to delegate disciplinary powers to others. Tupper noted it was absurd that, with all his other concerns, the chief had to deal with mundane matters such as dress infractions. It was an intolerable and humiliating situation that Mulligan had endured, and it must be changed. The ex-chief had pushed for more police. Tupper commented that the number of police could be raised immediately, as the present number of 713 was 22 less than the authorized 735. Tupper sharply criticized city council for its "mistaken policy" of holding down police costs, particularly when the crime rate was rising.

All those cleared by Tupper—police, politicians, bookies, and bootleggers—gave a large collective sigh of relief. Some commented, some didn't. Some who had been worried to death during the proceedings said they had known all along they had done nothing wrong and would be found innocent.

Many were glad Mulligan didn't take the stand to tell all he knew about his seven years as chief. Although he left the force under a cloud, many before him had also been ousted from office. It is impossible to judge whether he was any better or any worse than his predecessors. He held the position longer than had any of the 17 chiefs who preceded him as heads of a force with a troubled history—a history that, to be fair, was interspersed with periods of excellence and pride.

18. Sunny California

*I wondered if perhaps the press had decided to give us a
break and let us put it all behind us.*

Walter Mulligan

A veil of silence fell quickly on the Mulligan Affair, like the curtain at the end of a three-act play. The players had occupied centre stage and had said their piece. A consensus that enough was enough was shared by police, lawyers, politicians, bookies, and bootleggers alike. Losses of memory and stonewalling by witnesses had prevented Tupper from getting to the bottom of the scandal. His report left much that was murky. Surprisingly, there was little follow-up by the media and what there was was done without enthusiasm or a desire to uncover more. Even editorial criticism flagged, as everyone waited to see what Bonner's three-man committee would say.

No one had less to say than Mulligan. *Sun* reporter Jack Brooks tracked him down in sunny California and found him working for Rosedale Nurseries, about 20 miles from Los Angeles. A man who spent most of his life in uniform, Mulligan had traded police blue for the green jacket and fawn pants of his new employer. He was watering camellias when the newsman talked to him. "I always liked gardening, got a green thumb I suppose," commented Mulligan. He added that his new boss knew all about his background. That was about as much as he would say. He refused further comment on Tupper's report until he had seen a full copy, and he would not look at the one the reporter offered him. After this first encounter he declined to speak to the tide of persistent reporters that followed. He even changed jobs to try to shake them off.

Six months after he fled, Mulligan got the news that he had been waiting and hoping for. A *Province* headline summed up the findings of the three-man committee that studied the case. It said: "Evidence Not The Right Kind." The Attorney General's Office ruled , on July 31, 1956, that it didn't have sufficient evidence to support Tupper's findings of corruption and could not take the case to court. The statement meant that Mulligan was free to return to Canada whenever he pleased and that he would not be extradited. A spokesman for the Attorney General's Office said: "That is that, barring an unexpected break. But we anticipate that the whole case is closed." No one found a break, and Mulligan was never charged with a crime.

Walter Mulligan and his wife, Violet, who stood by him during the ordeal, remained in the US for over seven years. Two years after he knew there would be no prosecution, he changed uniforms again. This time Mulligan wore the garb of a coach company. He was a limousine-bus dispatcher at the Los Angeles airport. True to his inherent ambition, he worked his way up the company ladder and, in less than two years, had responsibility for a staff of 20. Those working for him found him "happy and cheerful," with a great sense of humour. He was well liked. His boss, J.R. Britton of Airport Coach Services, went further, saying Mulligan was one of the best-liked men in the limousine business.

Despite his seeming success in California, Mulligan missed police work and British Columbia. He applied for some security jobs, but background checks always turned up the history of the probe and that ended his chances. In May 1963, however, he quietly returned to Canada and took up residence and retirement in the Victoria suburb of Oak Bay. Even when his reappearance was discovered by the media, it was largely ignored. Mulligan, the centre of the storm eight years before, was now yesterday's news, a spent force. He hadn't talked, he hadn't been charged, and public interest had waned.

When confronted by *Province* reporter Paddy Sherman, Mulligan, already back a couple of months, expressed surprise that he hadn't been approached sooner. "I wondered if perhaps the press had decided to give us a break and let us put it all behind us," he said with a grin. Mulligan held no bitterness, although he felt the inquiry was one-sided and unfair. He said he had waited for months to testify but finally, on the advice of his lawyer, gave up.

He had gone to California because he felt there was no chance of getting a job in Canada. He returned because he liked the country and felt it had been good to him, despite all he had gone through. Mulligan spent some of his spare time writing about his long career as a policeman, although his reminiscences were never published. He had chosen Oak Bay as a place to live because he believed reporters would have hounded him in the Lower Mainland. However, Oak Bay isn't that far from Vancouver. If the media had been interested they would have made the trip.

Walter Mulligan spent his last years enjoying one of his professed life-long loves—gardening. He lived quietly. Even at the peak of his career, Mulligan had never been ostentatious or a big spender. Douglas, the ex-mistress, told the probe he acted like one, although her list of what he gave her hardly bore this out. When he died in Oak Bay in May 1987, there was only a handful of people at his funeral. Walter and Violet had no children. The man who had dominated the news, the centre of British Columbia's biggest story of 1955, got very brief obituaries. He was all but forgotten; fame and infamy were both fleeting.

After his exodus to the US Mulligan found a way to remain in uniform. He proved both resilient and pragmatic, accepting the occasional visit from Vancouver's press as part of his life.

19.   In Retrospect—40 Years Later

When Mulligan quit the Tupper Inquiry, *Sun* columnist Barry Mather wrote a poem he called "Police Probe News in Brief."

> *Off Again,*
> *On Again,*
> *Gone Again,*
> *Mulligan.*

In a more serious vein, a *Sun* editorial questioned the use of the Royal Commission process: "The attorney general may have to acknowledge his own share of the blame. It seems to have been a case of too much haste in launching the inquiry without previous investigation of what might be involved. Had the attorney general looked more carefully before he leapt, he might have ordered a different procedure to attain the desired end."

Even for its time, the Tupper Inquiry was not overly expensive. The commissioner was paid tribute in Victoria when he billed for $15,000, a figure much lower than what was expected. Costs have gone up, however, and in April 1997 the Somalia Inquiry had already cost taxpayers about $24 million. In the words of Canadian political historian Jack Granetstein of the University of Toronto (who was quoted on national television following the conclusion of the Somalia hearings), a commission of inquiry is introduced "to shelve a problem" not to solve it. It seems not much has changed in 45 years.

Four of the players in the Mulligan Affair, who were at the start of prominent careers as the Royal Commission opened in 1955, look back on these days as a great beginning, an experience that helped set them on successful roads. Each was young, new on the job, and destined to be influential in the life and times of British Columbia. They are today each celebrated in the fields of law, politics, and the media. They are H.A.D. Oliver, Stewart McMorran, Jack Webster, and Robert Bonner, and their stories follow.

If you're pestered by critics and hounded by faction
To take some precipitate positive action
The proper procedure to take my advice is
Appoint a Commission and stave off the crisis.
By shelving the matter you daunt opposition
And blunt its impatience by months of attrition
Replying meanwhile with a shrug and a smile
"The matter's referred to a Royal Commission."

A Royal Commission is strictly impartial,
The pros and the cons it will expertly martial
And one of its principal characteristics
Is getting bogged down in a sea of statistics.
So should you, perhaps, for inaction be chided
An answer to all men is aptly provided;
You simply explain, again and again,
"The Royal Commission has not yet decided."

Let the terms of its reference lack proper precision
That arguments lengthy may hold up decision,
And then, while they fumble with fact and with figure,
The conflict within the Commission grows bigger
And so, when at last its report is provided,
You say with a pout "The matter's in doubt,
The Royal Commission is somewhat divided."

Thus once a Commission its session commences,
All you have to do is sit on your fences
No longer in danger of coming a cropper
For prejudging its findings is highly improper.
When the subject's been held for so long in suspension
That it ceases to call forth debate and dissension,
Announce without fuss "There's no more to discuss,
The Royal Commission's retired on a pension."

If delay quite indefinite be your endeavour,
There's nothing to stop the thing sitting forever,
Til its members, worn out by their manifold rigours
Die off, one by one, like the ten little niggers.
Though, shrouded with cobwebs, a sight for compunction,
A few frail survivors may labour with unction
If somebody asked why, they'd sadly reply,
"The Royal Commission's forgotten its function."

Even before the departure of the key figure, the Sun *had reprinted a piece from Britain's* Punch *magazine—a piece that epitomized editorial opinion at the time and that, in large measure, had the approval of the general public.*

Judge H.A.D. Oliver

Reggie held the scales of justice with an even but inexperienced hand.

H.A.D. Oliver

A phone call from the police union was lawyer "Had" Oliver's introduction to the Tupper Inquiry and the beginning of his key role as the defence counsel for Len Cuthbert. Recently arrived from England, Oliver had quickly established a reputation as an experienced, confident, capable, and scrappy criminal lawyer, respectful of, but not awed by, the judges of the Vancouver courts (with whom he had some spectacular run-ins).

"It was all so long ago," he mused as he reminisced about the affair, which, as it had for Jack Webster, helped stamp his identity and enhance his reputation in British Columbia. Retired from the bench in 1996, not of his own choosing but because he had reached the age of 75, Oliver was back with his law firm in a high-rise office directly across Hornby Street from the old court house where the Mulligan drama had played itself out.

He chose criminal law as his field shortly after he arrived in Vancouver. He had the requisite experience and needed to make some money as quickly as possible. There were currency restrictions for those leaving England, and he noted with a laugh that the initial fee to get into the BC Law Society took most of it. "It was intended to keep out English lawyers," he joked.

Some judges saw Had Oliver as an uppity Brit who needed knocking down, and some of his fellow lawyers felt the same; but none doubted his ability. The Bentley-driving Oliver took it all in stride and, possibly just to annoy people, affected even more the image of the smooth, erudite, scholarly British barrister so often portrayed in television and movies. Today the English accent is not as pronounced as it was, the Bentley has been rear-ended and replaced by a Rolls Royce—"25-years-old and a bit long in the tooth"—and he now looks back on a life that included serving as consul for Liberia and as BC president of the International Wine and Food Society. He is humourous and a good story-teller, and he has an impeccable command of the English language.

Appreciating that it's good for a criminal lawyer to hang his shingle out where the crime is, Had Oliver originally set up shop at Main and Cordova, near the old police station and skid row. He had the second floor of a grotty old bank building. Rank-and-file cops and reporters covering crime soon got to know him. It was this connection that led him to the Tupper Inquiry, and he is now one of the last survivors of those who played a major role in the 1955 spectacle.

The police union asked him to represent Len Cuthbert. "I had met him casually through courtroom work," Oliver recalled. "We all thought it would be a relatively short affair and I set a fee accordingly." Seven months later, the fee didn't match the time put in.

"Cuthbert was a very pleasant guy. He was one of the nicest people you could hope to meet, not the stereotype of a policeman. He was a gentle soul," reflected Oliver, emphasizing that criminal defence lawyers don't always like their clients. He broke his usual practice and met with Cuthbert and his family. "I liked them," he added. "It was probably correct to say that Cuthbert was easily swayed and fell under Mulligan's domination."

Oliver had met Mulligan at a couple of social events and had one of his celebrated run-ins over the treatment accorded to two of Oliver's clients, who had been arrested. "Mulligan was not a man who readily admitted he was wrong," recalled the retired judge. Oliver scrapped with others, too, over legal differences or unfairness. He remembers well an argument with Police Commissioner Rey Sargent. After the dust settled, "we never did get on terribly well."

Choosing his words carefully, as is his wont, Oliver said that Reggie Tupper was "a most honourable man, the most capable solicitor you could ever want to meet, most courteous and kindly." The only problem was, noted the judge, "he didn't know where the court house was." Oliver agreed with the common view that Tupper lacked the necessary experience in the courtroom and in criminal work to undertake a commission of this kind. "Why Bonner picked him I will never know," he said. "A more experienced attorney general would have got one of the lawyers well known as experienced in this work." Oliver said the inquiry would have been over much sooner if such a person had been commissioner. He stressed, however, that he was "sure [Tupper] did his very best to be fair to everybody and his rulings on admissibility of evidence were what he believed to be correct, a view not necessarily shared by anybody else." Oliver smilingly summed it up: "Reggie held the scales of justice with an even but inexperienced hand."

A veteran of Royal Commissions both in Canada and the UK, Oliver is not a fan of such means of investigation, and he pointed to the Somalia probe as an example of why. He pointed out that Royal Commissioners are entitled to hear hearsay evidence, "which I always thought was unfair." He said that evasions and "convenient memory" can be expected if statements may later be used in evidence against witnesses. He is wary of politicians' agendas and, personally, would much sooner take his chances with a judge than with a commission.

Reflecting on the performance of the Police Commission during Mulligan's reign as chief, Oliver commented: "They probably did their job in keeping with the standards of the times, which were not very good."

During his long career as a criminal lawyer, Oliver said he always recognized the value of knowing and having friends in the media. He looked back with fondness to his sessions with Jack Webster, Jack Wasserman, Ed Moyer, and the others of the era who covered crime. He knew how to play the game, he knew the deadlines for editions and broadcasts, and he knew the reporters' need for news. "If the opportunity existed about 20 minutes before his radio deadline I always tried to get something for Jack," he smiled.

The judge's recognition of a stout defence—no loopholes for the other side—came through even when he recalled the demise of his beloved Bentley, rear-ended on a Vancouver street by a woman driving a small Japanese car. The Bentley was slightly damaged, while her car looked like a concertina. Nobody was hurt. The judge said a nearby resident invited them into her house to await police and asked if they'd like a nerve-steadying drink. "I declined, preferring to wait until after the investigation," said Had Oliver.

In 1997, H.A.D. Oliver was appointed by the provincial government to become BC's second Conflict of Interest Commissioner succeeding Ted Hughes. His interview for this story was conducted before his acceptance of that position.

Stewart McMorran had a distinguished career as both city prosecutor and judge. His personal scrapbook of 1955-6, compiled primarily by his late wife remains an intriguing record of Vancouver journalism.

Judge Stewart McMorran

> *He was alright as long as you knew when to say stop, and*
> *I could do that, at least part of the time.*
>
> Stewart McMorran on Ray Munro

"Evidence, some corroborated evidence was all that was needed to nail Mulligan. They knew he was crooked, but knowing and proving were two different things." Today, more than 40 years later, it still irks Stewart McMorran that the chief got off scott free. Looking back he is critical of the Mounties called in to investigate and has some quite uncomplimentary observations to make about Inspector Dube, who was authorized by Attorney General Bonner to pursue alleged criminal activities mentioned in the Tupper Inquiry. "With all that was going on, the bookies and the bootleggers involved, it's hard to imagine they couldn't find something or somebody who would talk," said McMorran, as he sat in his penthouse suite overlooking False Creek and Vancouver's skyline. But they didn't.

Silver-haired, slim, and dapper at 78, McMorran was just beginning his career when the Mulligan Affair burst on the scene. It was a milestone in a career that took him from lawyer to city prosecutor to county court judge. Vancouver-born, he attended UBC before joining the army in the Second World War. He recalls vividly one of his first meetings with Tupper, who was the university's Dean of Law. When McMorran applied to return to his studies after the war, Tupper, always the stickler for protocol, ruled that he must rewrite all his exams. McMorran had to rewrite 29 exams in three months in order to maintain his standing—a challenge he met successfully. Tupper was a man he would always remember. McMorran spent close to 30 years in the rough-and-tumble of Vancouver's court system before becoming a county court judge in 1974, a position he held for almost 20 years before retiring in the 1990s.

At the beginning of his career, in order to gain experience, he worked for free in the prosecutor's office. This was an apprenticeship of sorts. Then he was employed as assistant city prosecutor until January 1954, when he was appointed to replace Gordon Scott in the city prosecutor's office. The salary range, as stated in the Police Commission minutes, was $800 to $960 per month, a substantial salary at that time. It was slightly more than Mulligan made as Vancouver's top cop, with 27 years' service on the force. When he stepped in to take over, McMorran was well aware of the mounting crisis in the police department and the allegations concerning Mulligan's activities.

The prosecutor's office was located in police headquarters on Main Street, only a floor above the department brass. There were daily conversations about crime, how cases were being handled, and general concerns regarding the department. Over the years McMorran gained the trust and respect of many policemen, particularly of Bob Leatherdale and Archie Plummer. "There were a lot like them, but there also were many totally under Mulligan's sway," he remembered. He recalled the chief as a man with a tremendous personality and presence who "spoke well, better than any of the other chiefs I knew." He was also a man with great persuasive powers and didn't hesitate to use them on those he wanted to influence. "Cuthbert was a pushover, he shouldn't have been leading the gambling squad. He was a follower," McMorran maintained.

Mulligan's former mistress, Helen Douglas, was another person that the chief held in thrall. "At first she didn't want to come. A lot of people knew about her and Mulligan, but nobody had talked much," McMorran said, "It would be a whole different story today." He felt that she was "frightened to death, she was scared stiff of Walter Mulligan."

McMorran smiled as he thought of Ray Munro, noting that he had a soft spot in his heart for the irrepressible reporter. "He was alright as long as you knew when to say stop, and I could do that, at least part of the time," he joked. Munro obviously felt he had a lot of pull with the prosecutor because of an absurd proposal—the kind only Munro could make. He asked McMorran to wear a wire when he went to see Attorney General Robert Bonner. The prosecutor pretended to go along with the suggestion. When McMorran met Bonner in Victoria, he told the attorney general that his timepiece was really a recording device. "I thought Bonner would go crazy," he laughed. Needless to say, Munro didn't get his taped conversation.

Evidence of what McMorran thought was the good side of Ray Munro hangs in the library of his penthouse. It consists of three framed pictures, in sequence, of the event that won Munro a National Newspaper Award for photography. They show an irate Canada goose flying up to attack a policeman and his horse in Stanley Park. There was a suggestion that Munro talked the cop into riding near the nesting goose in the hope that it would respond. With Munro's luck, it did.

Tupper was a good lawyer, a dignified, reasonable man in McMorran's opinion. He was appointed to head a difficult and controversial inquiry without having had much actual experience with courtroom work and the complexities of evidence and cross-examination. "It wasn't a trial. There was a lot of hearsay evidence, as there is in inquiries. Today we've got the Somalia commission," McMorran noted. "It's like walking on eggs. Somebody comes up with something and everybody believes it. Tupper couldn't do much about it. He did the best he could."

Tupper wanted McMorran as chief counsel, but it was a job he couldn't take because of his role as city prosecutor. He was advised by Magistrate Orr and others that he would be in an invidious position because he had worked behind the scenes collecting evidence. For many months before the crisis broke, he met with potential witnesses and listened to Jack Whelan, while trying to find corroboration for Len Cuthbert's allegations. He continued his work of identifying potential witnesses until it was formally announced, two months after the probe began, that he was returning full-time to his city prosecutor's job.

As one member of the three-man committee appointed to review inquiry evidence and the special report of RCMP inspector Dube, McMorran still shows his frustration at the lack of solid evidence uncovered. Such evidence was essential if a case against Mulligan, Cuthbert, and the bookies was to be taken to court. The Dube investigation, which lasted for months and was ongoing throughout the Tupper Inquiry, was also backed by hundreds of interviews conducted by commission counsel. McMorran believes that the Mounties, on this occasion, came up very short. There was nothing in the report that would convict anyone. For what it didn't contain, or possibly for what it might have revealed concerning the scope of the scandal, the Dube Report was never made public, and, to this day, nobody in the Attorney General's Office knows anything about it. The Tupper Report is filed in the provincial archives in Victoria, but the Dube Report is not with it.

Despite disappointment at the outcome, and the fact that no one went to jail for the graft and corruption reported by Tupper, McMorran notes philosophically: "At best it cleared the air for the Vancouver Police Department, at least for a few years." He believes the choice of George Archer to replace Walter Mulligan as chief was a good one. Archer, the veteran RCMP superintendent, was a strict disciplinarian, something McMorran considers to have been vital to reorganizing the Vancouver Police Department in 1956. Today, said McMorran, battling crime is so much more sophisticated and complex than it was 40 years ago. The veteran lawyer, prosecutor, and BC Supreme Court judge believes that the Vancouver police of the late 1990s are doing a good job against tough opposition.

Honorable Robert Bonner

The real problem was keeping the Commission out of the hands of local politicians.

Robert Bonner

Cronyism is the curse of politics at all levels and it had a major effect on life in Vancouver and British Columbia during the Walter Mulligan era. It's what happens when "everybody knows everybody else too well to be objective," said Robert Bonner, 76, sitting in his West-Side Vancouver home recalling the days when he was the province's attorney general, its chief law enforcer. Bonner held the post for Premier W.A.C. Bennett's Social Credit government from 1952 until he retired from politics in 1968. He was the closest political confidant Premier Bennett had in his Cabinet. Bonner recalled that they lunched together almost every day during the Socreds' long reign. It's not surprising! "Wacky" and his boys had more than their share of troubles, all of which called for legal advice. Bob Bonner went on to become chairman and chief executive officer of lumber company giant McMillan-Bloedel and then chairman of BC Hydro.

Bonner freely admits that it was the same old cronyism that led to the recent demise of Social Credit. In the 1990s the Socreds became the kind of government they had swept out of power in 1952. They paid the price for mutual back-rubbing.

A Seaforth Highlander in the Second World War and a member of the first post-war graduating law class from UBC, Bonner started his political life as a Tory. When Bennett scored an upset victory in 1952, he had a lot of bench strength in the world of small business, but there wasn't a lawyer in the bunch. Three months later Bennett talked Bonner into running in a by-election, which he won handily. The premier appointed him attorney general and he retained the position for the next 16 years, the only top law man Bennett ever had in his Cabinet. There weren't many people Bonner didn't know on the political, legal, and law-enforcement scene during those years. Though out of the limelight for many years, Bonner is still the old political pro.

The Vancouver Police Department in the 1940s and early 1950s, he noted with a laugh, was regarded as "part of the Liberal Party." His predecessor as attorney general was, of course, the swinging Gordon Wismer.

Bonner confessed that he didn't remember too many details of the Mulligan Affair. He had probably met the chief on several occasions at various events but had no recollection of him. When he was approached by the Police

Commission in 1955 with a request for an inquiry, he quickly ordered one. When the confessions started to pour out about criminal activity he agreed, again at the request of the Police Commission, to bring in the RCMP to investigate. At no time was there any indication that Bonner had any direct involvement in the affair. The details of the case were delegated to departmental officials, for whom he still has the highest praise.

Bonner had other things to worry about during the Mulligan Affair, which he described as more of a local Vancouver issue. In mid-1955 a major scandal broke in the Legislature over charges of bribery with regard to the granting of forest-management licences. The Socred government ducked and weaved as long as it could, but finally Lands and Forests Minister Robert Sommers resigned. After a lengthy and colourful trial he went to jail. The Sommers case had more political significance and importance for the Socred government than did wrong-doing in the Vancouver Police Department.

Bob Bonner disagreed with the view that Tupper suffered from a lack of courtroom experience in his role as commissioner. "You're not always elected because you know something about the job," said Bonner with a chuckle. He felt that Tupper had a keen, inquiring mind and that was the key factor in running a Royal Commission.

As he had stated during the Mulligan Affair, Bonner found nothing wrong with Tupper's handling of the inquiry. He added that he did not see the report by Inspector Dube but had every confidence in the three-man committee's decision that there was not sufficient evidence to take Mulligan to trial.

Bonner made a comment regarding the use of Royal Commissions in general and Canada's most recent one in particular. As an outside observer, he felt that a major problem of the recent Somalia Inquiry in Ottawa was the commission counsel's lack of drive in mustering evidence and pushing it through. "They seem to have a roomful of lawyers wandering around at $150-an-hour, letting everything fly out to see what lands." He felt that there were similarities between the Tupper and the Somalia Inquiries regarding their inability to provide a foundation for criminal proceedings. In his mind there was much to be learned from the US system of senate hearings and special prosecutors when tackling such investigations.

The former attorney general said he had great respect for the professionalism of the RCMP during the Mulligan era. Bonner noted the same could not be said for how he felt about the Vancouver police. The Tupper Inquiry did lead to much higher standards for city police recruitment and training. Bonner pointed to the addition of former military men to the Police Commission as a key to pushing through improvements. With no criticism of the performance of the 1950s commission, Bonner stressed that "the real problem was keeping the commission out of the hands of local politicians," which brought him back to his point on cronyism.

An Autobiography by Jack Webster

Starting in 1952 Robert Bonner was attorney general of British Columbia for 16 years and a highly visible business executive afterwards. In 1976 he became chairman of BC Hydro. Keeping a low profile after retiring a decade later, he still practices law. He was recently quoted as saying: "Nobody had heard of me much before 1952 and not much since 1986."

Jack Webster offered his candid assessment of many personalities involved in the Mulligan Affair in his autobiography, published by Douglas & McIntyre in 1990. When R.H. Tupper refused his request to broadcast the inquiry live from the courtroom, Jack reverted to his expert knowledge of Pitman shorthand to record and re-enact proceedings.

Jack Webster

Vancouver was wide open, there was a lot of graft. A lot of
cops were on the take. Drugs were really only beginning.

                                                        Jack Webster

A widower living alone in a view home on Vancouver's expensive west side, Webster, 79, is also the laird of 90 acres of former sheep farm on Salt Spring Island, largest of the Gulf Islands lying between the Lower Mainland and Vancouver Island in Georgia Strait. Both of them were made possible by the career that the feisty Scotsman carved out for himself following the Mulligan Affair, which he acknowledges "made my mark in Vancouver." Columnist Al Fotheringham delighted in designating Webster the "oatmeal savage."

For more than 30 years Webster dominated Vancouver's air waves on both radio and television. He knew the rich, famous, and powerful well, eventually becoming one of them himself. He was one of the few, the very few, newspeople that former prime minister Pierre Trudeau liked. Webster set his own salary on his TV news and public affairs show, and his autobiography, published in 1990, sold 50,000 copies. Latterly he was one of the panel on the seemingly unending *Front Page Challenge* TV show. It ended, grumbled a crotchety Webster, when some young whippersnapper producer wanted to make it more controversial.

He recalled the countless hours he spent during the Tupper Inquiry "among the spiders and steampipes" in the basement of the Grosvenor Hotel, where CJOR had its studio. Some broadcasts lasted five hours, going well into the night. Webster held much of British Columbia captive as he read his verbatim notes of the revelations and related the unfolding drama of the inquiry. Tupper had ruled out taping the proceedings, and Webster made the most of his shorthand. Webster had a broadcast at noon, another in the afternoon, and then, after six at night, he began his blow-by-blow account of the entire day's events. It was a brilliant performance. No shrinking violet, Webster would back up this endorsement. Canny Scot that he is, he noted that he got a nice tax write-off when he turned over the tapes of his own broadcasts to the provincial archives. The notebooks are no more, lost in one of his many moves from office to home to new home and back again.

Webster remembered with a grin that, during the inquiry, he loved to irritate Vancouver's dailies, starting every broadcast with the statement that listeners were about to hear a story that they wouldn't read in the *Sun* or the *Province* "today, tomorrow or the day after." Actually, that was not true. Caught sleeping originally, the two main papers provided massive coverage, column after column, of the proceedings. Some of it was trivia that could have been eliminated, although the *Sun* sometimes referred to it as a "word-by-word" account of what went on. Some of the reporters observed that Webster was sometimes out of the court during the proceedings and wryly commented that he had scalped some of their verbatim coverage for his broadcast.

Webster recalled that "Vancouver was wide open, there was a lot of graft. A lot of cops were on the take. Drugs were really only beginning." He also held the view that *Province* reporter Eddie Moyer had the best police contacts in town and passed on information to Munro, who finally found a market for his stories. The writing was wild and extravagant and full of mistakes and innuendo, commented Webster, but with enough facts to help topple Mulligan's applecart.

The inquiry meandered. "Even the allegations were difficult to pin down. It was all maybes and perhaps[es]. Cops saying I can't remember, I don't recall. It was a whitewash," Webster maintained. The policeman who emerged clean and most believable was Bob Leatherdale. "He was offered to be cut in on graft but he turned it down," Webster said. In his book, he wrote: "The inquiry was an exercise in damage control. The legal and political establishment in Vancouver wanted to restrict the effects of the scandal and play down its implications. To be fair, Tupper was overwhelmed by tentative, guarded and qualified answers. He still fudged it all in a report that was duller than dishwasher."

Jack Webster and Walter Mulligan had a certain respect for each other, and Webster was one of the very few reporters the ex-chief talked to after he returned to Canada. The broadcaster visited Mulligan in Victoria, and the former chief welcomed him civilly to his house. It was different with Violet. Webster recalled that when she saw him, she screamed: "Jack Webster, you ruined my life! Get out of here! Get the hell out of here!" Webster got out without hesitation.

Like McMorran, Webster believes that the probe never really got down to a full assessment of how deep the graft and corruption reached, but at least it chopped off the rot at the top and cleaned up the department at the time.

20. Winners and Losers

There's no dough left in bootlegging. All the bawdyhouses
are closed. Now they stop a man taking a few honest bets.
Joe Celona

Like phoney wars, whitewashes leave few casualties. In life-and-death terms, there was really only one death in the Mulligan Affair and he was innocent. Superintendent Harry Whelan was never implicated in the torrent of testimony about graft and corruption. Tormented and torn by the events and the evidence he would have to give, his only crime was turning his gun on himself.

His brother Jack, the former cop and sometime partner of Walter Mulligan in the Piggy Bank caper, was less than Simon Pure. He received no censure from Tupper, but the commissioner had doubts and suspicions about Jack Whelan, whom he called an unreliable witness.

The commissioner named only four men as directly involved in graft— cops Walter Mulligan and Len Cuthbert and bookies Pete Wallace and George Sutherland. Tupper said he had doubts about other members of Cuthbert's gambling squad but that lack of supporting evidence made it impossible to indict them.

Most of the senior policemen involved were veterans, not far from retirement in 1955. For them the Mulligan Affair was their 15 minutes in the spotlight—a spotlight some found uncomfortable. It was enough to encourage them to seek relative obscurity for the remainder of their careers. The inquiry had no apparent impact on their professional lives; it was as though nothing had happened.

New police chief George Archer accepted his senior mens' testimony to the effect that they were not involved. In the shakeup that followed his appointment, Gordon Ambrose, former assistant chief constable, became deputy chief in charge of operations. Alan Rossiter, the temporary chief during the probe, became staff superintendent. Superintendent Jack Horton was put in charge of detectives, and Inspector Pete Lamont, who denied everything during the probe, headed the General Investigation Division. Sergeant Bob Leatherdale remained in Lamont's division and Sergeant Archie Plummer was named to handle narcotics in the vice detail. The reorganization took place before the release of the Tupper Report.

Only Cuthbert lost his job, although some did not advance up the ladder as they might have done had the inquiry not taken place. Their only loss was one of self-esteem and the respect of the public. Len Cuthbert's career ended in the spring of 1956 with his dismissal upon the ruling that his attempted suicide contravened police regulations. He worked briefly as the night clerk in a cheap hotel, and then friends found him a security job with a new company that moved into town. In 1969 he was a chipper 68 when he posed for a *Sun* photograph at an auction, where he bought an antique fire hydrant. His former notoriety was neither mentioned nor, obviously, did it worry him. He lived to a ripe old age.

Mulligan's mistress, Helen Douglas, disappeared from the scene completely. Her married name and the identity of her husband were never disclosed.

Cynics might say that, as always, the lawyers were the big winners. Most picked up large fees and enough publicity to enhance their reputations and future careers. Tupper was lauded by the provincial government, and his law firm became one of the largest and best known in Vancouver. He died in 1972.

A number of lawyers involved in the Mulligan Affair went on to the bench, where their names became well known and appeared regularly in the newspapers as they sat in judgement over both minor and major crimes. These included Tom Norris, J.G.A Hutcheson, Angelo Branca, Jay Gould, Nick Mussallem, and Vic Dryer. Gordon Scott, who was a witness during the inquiry, also became a judge.

The police commissioners (i.e., Mayor Charles Thompson, Mayor Fred Hume, Magistrate Oscar Orr, and Judge Rey Sargent) all lived out their lives in their chosen fields and received fitting public eulogies when they died, as did former attorney general Gordon Wismer. As testimony revealed, and as Tupper commented, the police commissioners' handling of Mulligan following Len Cuthbert's 1949 confession was irresponsible. They should have taken immediate action. Tupper found that there were many unanswered questions concerning their reasoning and actions. Despite his comments they carried on, their reputations untarnished.

Among the reporters were headliners and future politicians. Ray Munro went on to various careers, mostly in aviation. He was awarded the Order of Canada in 1973 for his work in promoting Canada's Aviation Hall of Fame. At one time he toured the country as "The Great Raymond," a hypnotist who drew audiences in most large Canadian cities. Reporters recalled him practising hypnosis on the copy boys during his years at the *Province*. Later he became a lecturer, speaking to executives about mastering fear, another subject in which he claimed expertise. He was always on the hunt for publicity but never again made the spectacular headlines he created before and during the Mulligan Affair in Vancouver.

Ray Munro was 72 when he died of cancer in Toronto in June 1994. He left five children. One of the great personal tragedies of his life was the suicide of his oldest son.

Wasserman went on to fame and fortune as a TV talk show host after leaving the *Sun*. Always a popular performer, he died with a flourish in 1977 while speaking at a roast honouring his old friend, colourful crusty millionaire timber baron Gordon Gibson. Many laughed when Wasserman took a prat fall off the stage; they thought it was all part of his schtick, but it wasn't. He died of a heart attack at the age of 50, and Vancouver lost one of its leading characters. Hundreds attended his funeral, which was different, even for a Winnipeg-born Jewish boy. It was held in a Unitarian Church, a rabbi sang, and a pipe band played "Amazing Grace." A woman was escorted out when she started shouting that if he hadn't been making jokes about Roman Catholics at the roast he would still be alive. It would have made a great Wasserman column.

Another who died too soon was former *Province* police reporter Eddie Moyer, a man who knew Mulligan better than most, who left the newspaper business for public relations. He handled media relations for the Pacific National Exhibition until his death from cancer in 1964 at the age of 44. *Province* gossip columnist Dan Ekman, who was strong competition for Wasserman, also entered public relations, spending much of his life as a political consultant. Fortunately, unlike his colleagues, he lived a long and productive life.

Four reporters who were prominent on the *Sun* and the *Province* during the 1950s became so involved in public concerns that they decided to throw their hats in the ring as politicians. Columnist Barry Mather was the first to earn a seat as a New Democratic Party MP. Simma Holt held a one-term seat for the Liberals during Pierre Trudeau's reign, as did Paul St Pierre, a *Sun* writer and author. In 1980 Pat Carney took the Vancouver Centre seat for the Conservative party and held it throughout Prime Minister Brian Mulroney's reign before being appointed to the Senate.

It would be too much like the mission hall conversion scene at the close of *Guys and Dolls* to believe that Vancouver's bootleggers and bookies saw the light after the Mulligan Affair. None of them again made the kind of headlines they did during the seven months of the probe. Nevertheless, in

Vancouver the cards were still dealt, the dice were still rolled, and the racing tip sheets were still sold.

The oldest established crook, who had been in the vice business since the 1920s, remained unrepentent. Joe Celona died at age 60 in 1968. He had one more minor brush with the law after the Mulligan Affair and then threw in his hand. He told a reporter: "There's no dough left in bootlegging. All the bawdyhouses are closed. Now they stop a man taking a few honest bets." He knew enough to fold when the odds were against him.

21. Different Days Different Cops

Vancouver hasn't picked an outsider since chief Walter Mulligan was bounced for corruption in 1955 to be replaced by RCMP Superintendent George Archer.

The Province

Almost 40 years after a disgraced Walter Mulligan fled into exile in the United States, another Vancouver police chief came a cropper in yet another provincial inquiry into wrong-doing. William Marshal resigned in 1993 when he was found responsible for not properly investigating the alleged assault of a prisoner in the city jail a decade earlier. His offence was minor and justice was swift compared to what happened with Mulligan, but he, too, lost a job he cherished.

Marshal's sudden departure left an unexpected vacancy at the top for Ray Canuel, who never expected to be top cop because in 1993 he was only four years from mandatory retirement. In the police department it seems that history *does* repeat itself, and on at least two occasions a top cop near retirement proved to be outstanding. Canuel accounts for one of these and the man who followed Mulligan accounts for the other. RCMP superintendent George Archer was due to retire when he was asked to head up the Vancouver force. He is referred to in the police history as one of the best.

Crime remains a problem in Vancouver, and newspaper headlines have not changed much in 45 years, although policing has. In mid-1997, the *Sun*'s headlines have a certain similarity to those of mid-1955: May 2, 1997, "New Board to Hear Public Complaints About Police"; May 8, "Vancouver Most Crime-Ridden Canadian City, Study Shows." In June the news was not much better: June 4, "A Top Cop's Top Job—Some Advice for Vancouver's New Chief of Police"; June 9, "Mayor Owen to Meet Justice Minister on Drug Laws."

Ray Canuel, Vancouver's retiring chief in 1997, was a graduate of the school of hard knocks, a former federal jail guard who joined the force in 1966 pretty close to the bottom. He was a turnkey in the old city slammer. Observers say that Canuel, as top cop, turned out to be a good old-style policeman capable of modern thinking.

The chief believed there was a need to return to the image of the strolling, whistling, friendly, mythical Officer Kelly, well known and wise to his beat. To keep up with new, sophisticated, and increasingly violent crime, there also had to be an educated, well-trained, responsive police department backed by the latest in equipment and technology. As a member of the old school he surprised and upset some old timers with his new business-like approach to policing. Spending was at a large-size corporation level, with two major problems: the police wanted more in personnel and equipment and the public complained that this was too expensive. Resources couldn't be wasted, optimum utilization and planning were paramount. Canuel decided that old rigid regulations and unquestioning discipline had to go because they hamstring individual initiative. On balance, Canuel achieved some of his goals in his relatively short reign.

He gave cops more flexibility. For example, they can now order cars towed away for infractions without having to get permission from a superior. To reach out more to the public he set up a citizens' advisory group and opened 10 community policing offices. Canuel favoured one unified force for the Lower Mainland. But that will be a long time coming because politicians believe the status quo serves them better. There are always local rivalries, and the maintenance of fiefdoms is important to some.

In 1997, Ray Canuel made about $150,000 a year in salary and benefits, more than 14 times what Mulligan made. A staff sergeant makes $90,000 and a 20-year cop about $77,000. A 10-year custodial guard earns $63,000. Tack on overtime and its more. A rookie probationer makes close to $44,000, a good reason there's a long line up of people waiting to join the force. Without a university degree or similar education, plus special qualifications and skills, there wasn't much chance of being one of the approximately 50 new members of the force in 1997.

Mulligan had about 700 personnel, Canuel 1,084, including 139 female officers, a much higher ratio than what existed in 1955. That's an increase of only 40 percent in 40 years, but the Vancouver force is now assisted by detachments of the RCMP and municipal forces, who patrol and police in the other 21 districts and municipalities of the Greater Vancouver Regional District. Mulligan's last budget was about $4 million. In 1997 Canuel's was $104 million.

In recent years Vancouver has received many immigrants, representing many cultures and lifestyles. Politicians try to put on a happy face: we're just one big understanding multicultural family getting on wonderfully well together. They'd rather not talk about some modern aspects of crime. Immigrants from certain violent, crime-ridden parts of the world, having different cultures and values from those endorsed in Canada, present new problems for the police. Only a small percentage of newcomers are in this category, but even one new gang is too many. And those who espouse the practices of dictators and despots in their former homelands are not acceptable.

The force has tried to recruit from the ethnic communities, both the old and the new, with varying results. Some newcomers have a built-in dislike and distrust of all police. On the force in 1997, however, were eight Native people (both male and female), along with officers of many other origins—3 African, 22 Chinese, 22 East Indians, 8 Japanese, 1 Thai, 1 Vietnamese, and 1 Filipino.

Along with the emergence of new racial gangs unknown in Mulligan's day, Vancouver police now face nine-year-old drug users, money laundering, an increase in the use of guns and other weapons, home invasions, credit card fraud, and an epidemic of cars stolen to meet the demands of illegal overseas markets.

To meet these new challenges Vancouver police in the 1990s have diversified, introducing specialists in a number of areas (such as child pornography, criminal harassment and stalking, arson, vehicle theft, forensic identification, computer fingerprinting, computer crime, criminal profiling, and so on). In some ways police have returned to 1886, when a cop pedalled a bike through Stanley Park on patrol. Vancouverites have become accustomed to bikes ridden by yellow-jacketed cops whizzing around town, weaving their way through gridlocked traffic. It's a sign of the times that during the day they can often move faster in response to emergency calls than can squad cars. In 10 years there have been no casualties among the biking cops, other than the odd bruised knee or elbow. On a nice summer day with a fresh breeze, and the opportunity to exercise while being paid, it's a popular job. About 60 are currently on the list, and there's no dearth of new volunteers.

The police union was asked for its comments on modern policing. As will be remembered, it was in the forefront of the battle against Mulligan and his methods all during his tenure. The union declined any comment.

Much has changed since Mulligan's time. The responsibility for the operation of the police department now lies with the Police Board, a group made up of the mayor (as chairman), who is the sole city council representative, along with six other members appointed at large from various occupations and walks of life (with attention paid to ethnic and gender representation). The present Police Commission operates out of the Attorney

General's Office in Victoria, setting certain standards and auditing budgets for police departments throughout the province. It was established by legislation in 1974.

In 1997 the groundwork was laid for meeting a major problem. Too many citizens felt the dice were heavily loaded against them when the police were responsible for investigating complaints against their own department. The establishment of a new independent civilian police commissioner was recommended by a two-year, $2 million study of policing headed by BC Supreme Court judge Wallace Oppal.

While many forms of gambling and provincial lotteries are now legal, one of the old problems persists and is now bigger than ever. As in Mulligan's time the spread of drugs continues to take its tragic toll, seemingly without a solution in sight. This battle is no nearer an end now than it was then. The police are smarter, better trained, and better paid. They still have internal problems but appear free of the sweeping graft and corruption prevalent in the Mulligan era, which is not to say all are eligible for sainthood.

In mid-1997, after six months, the search for a new chief ended. Police Chief Bruce Chambers moved from a small town with a small force to one of the most difficult positions in Canada. In Thunder Bay the annual budget was $36 million and the force numbered 518, in Vancouver the budget is $104 million and the force has increased to almost 1,100 members.

When Mulligan leapfrogged over many senior men to get the chief's job in 1947, he had already made many enemies in the department. Chief Chambers, while he had no old established antagonists, immediately acquired new critics. It wasn't only police officers who were unhappy with the Police Commission's choice; a veteran of various roles in the law business in Vancouver said it was a move that would severely shake morale. "Even if it turns out he is exceedingly smart and was much better than the other candidates, it means problems in the short term," he said.

Local officers know the new chief is well qualified, with 30 years experience and three university degrees, but reaction to the appointment was mixed. A *Province* story pointed out: "His selection—over four local candidates, including three deputy chiefs, on a short list of six—has caused mixed feelings." One senior officer found the decision to overlook the city's own talent "mystifying." According to another officer, "A decision like this is like a slap in the face . . . it's an affront to Canuel, who had little to do with the selection process and a concern for beat cops, who will bear the brunt of any transition period."

The new chief has a three-year contract with two-year extension options. His salary jumped to $129,500 a year from $110,000, which he received as police chief and general manager of the fire department in Thunder Bay. His comments when his appointment was made public included: "If you want to talk to me just pick up the phone and call." He says that he is not buffered by a layer of media officers. He is used to small-town responsiveness, and to prove it he phoned one local reporter four times before he got through.

Bruce Chambers said that a key focus for him would be community policing, which is already well established in Vancouver. He wanted to be sure there was a good balance between community policing and the more traditional reactive policing. His biggest challenge was "getting up to speed, getting a feel for the culture of the force."

Unfortunately, there wasn't much time for orientation. Chambers immediately faced the dissolution of Ports Canada Police, one of the largest security operations of its kind in Canada. In addition the Asia Pacific Economic Cooperation (APEC) Conference, whose attendees were scheduled to include President Bill Clinton and more than a dozen other heads of state, was set to occur within months of his appointment as police chief.

Mulligan may be gone, but he is not entirely forgotten. When doing a story about Chambers, one reporter commented: "Vancouver hasn't picked an outsider since chief Walter Mulligan was bounced for corruption in 1955 to be replaced by RCMP Superintendent George Archer."

The Authors

Ian Macdonald has worked on the *Victoria Colonist*, the *Vancouver Province* and the *Vancouver Sun*. He was legislative reporter for the *Sun* in Victoria for five years and Bureau Chief in Ottawa from 1965 to 1970. He worked in media relations for federal ministers, the prime minister and also as head of Transport Canada Information. He has written for magazines, radio, television and film.

Betty O'Keefe was a reporter on the *Province* for seven years in the mid-50s and later supervised corporate communications in Western Canada and the Western US, for a large Canadian corporation. Following this 15 year period she was commissioned to write two corporate biographies— *Brenda— The Story of a Mine* and *The Mines of Babine Lake*.

In 1994, Macdonald and O'Keefe decided to apply their journalistic talents to writing projects related to western Canadian history and contemporary issues. Their first book, published in 1996, was *The Klondike's 'Dear Little Nugget.'* A second book, *Earthquake, Your Chances, Your Options, Your Future*, was released in the fall of the same year. *The Mulligan Affair* is their third book. Ian and Betty are currently working on a book for Heritage centered on another historic incident in BC's past.

Acknowledgements

We acknowledge the courtesy of the following individuals and institutions in supplying photographs.

BCARS, 25 (top, bottom), 56 (bottom); City of Vancouver Archives, 10, 16 (bottom), 21, 27, 29; Himie Koshovey, 47 (bottom), 49 (bottom); Stewart McMorran, 142; H.A.D. Oliver, 142; Vancouver Public Library, 16 (centre), 83, 92; The *Vancouver Sun*, 16 (top), 18, 33, 64 (top), 77, 137; Jack Webster, 8, 47 (top), 148.